Triple Your
Intelligence—Now!

Triple Your Intelligence—Now!

Gene D. Matlock, B.A., M.A.

Authors Choice Press
San Jose New York Lincoln Shanghai

Triple Your Intelligence—Now!

Authors Choice Press
an imprint of iUniverse.com, Inc.

For information address:
iUniverse.com, Inc.
5220 S 16th, Ste. 200
Lincoln, NE 68512
www.iuniverse.com

In this book I often question and even mock many people's pet beliefs and theories. Those who have unusually delicate and pathological sensitivities must read at their own risk.

ISBN: 0-595-19975-5

Printed in the United States of America

Contents

Why I Absolutely Guarantee That You Can Triple Your Intelligence In As Little Time As One Day!

There are approximately two ways of measuring a person's intelligence. The first method is the normal I.Q. test in which a person's potential ability to learn and apply knowledge is measured. For example, when I was young, my I.Q. level was 120; not so high as I would like, but, as they say, we beggars can't be choosy.

The second method determines what percentage of a person's potential is being exploited advantageously. Scientists claim that average and below people use only two to five percent of their respective potentials. This is the most significant and valid method of testing intelligence, for how can a high I.Q. benefit a person who doesn't use it?

Another advantage of this second type of test is that it can be administered by untrained—even uneducated—personnel. All they have to do is observe a person to determine what he is doing with his life. Any individual should be able to devise his own battery of questions and administer the test to himself. For example, a person wanting to calculate what percentage of his intelligence he is using might want to include the following example questions as a small part of the total test:

1. Do I like to spend weekends drowning myself in beer and watching sports events?

2. While driving, do I like to drive fast and intimidate other drivers when I'm sure no policemen or highway patrolmen are nearby?

3. A good corollary to the above question would be, Do I police myself, or do I need policemen and religious authorities to force me to be a responsible member of society?

4. Do I belong to a religion emphasizing loud singing and clapping, energetic dancing and jumping, ear-splitting preaching, shouts, and banging of tambourines—or do I prefer one that emphasizes quiet meditation and serious introspection?

5. When I listen to music, must it destroy my auditory nerves and insult my intelligence—or do I want music that soothes, enlightens, and inspires?

6. When I suffer, do I ask why God allows good people to suffer—or do I accept any responsibility for what happens to me?

7. Do I want to be "just like everybody else," or do I want to be unique?

8. A corollary to question seven is, Who are the more unique of the two following groups: Those who like to wear weird clothing, tattoo their bodies, and dye their hair blue—or those whose moral and intellectual life separates them from the common herd?

9. Do I ask what my country can do for me—or what can I do for my country?

10. Many Black and Latino students accuse highly motivated students of their respective ethnicities of "acting white." What can you conclude from the following excerpt from an article that appeared in the 7-7-2001 edition of *The Los Angeles Times:* "Fights are not a problem at Fremont's Mission San Jose High School, where the student body is 61% minority, much of it Asian…'It's a real unique place to work. We rarely have discipline problems, said Principal Stuart Kew, who has seen the school evolve from predominantly white since he began there as a chemistry teacher in 1972. As the demographics have changed, so have the academics. The curriculum has become more advanced, because that is what the parents

and students want. Out of a student body of 2,000, a third are identified as gifted. 'There is a lot of inherent peer pressure at the school,' Kew said. 'There's a degree of parental pressure to take the hardest classes. But I think that a lot of dynamics in the student-body are self-imposed. The students compete against each other.' (***Asian Indians Remake Silicon Valley,*** by Bettina Boxall.)

Who acts "White" at Fremont's Mission San Jose High School?

The preceding are just a few example questions among the *hundred plus* you should ask yourself.

Now for the grading criteria: If you administer the test honestly, and just one question implies a deficiency, you are not living up to your expectations. You are using five percent or less of your total potential. Even though I am a leading exponent of this type of self-administered test, I'm sad to say that I have never been able to pass it to my satisfaction. Hopefully, you'll have better luck.

Since I have never made a high score on this test, some readers may question my qualifications for writing a book like this. But look at things this way: *No one is more stupid and irritating than a self-satisfied person.*

In this book, I will show you how to increase your chances of passing this test and tripling your mind power use to approximately fifteen percent of your potential, leaving about 85 percent in reserve—and in only one day! Yes, you can do it!

The following are some of the secrets you'll learn in the following chapters:

1. Learn how the incorrect definition and use of the word *Belief* is the direct cause of nearly all wars, tensions, misunderstandings, psychological difficulties, stupidity, ignorance, and broken lives. Hardly anyone, not even highly educated people, knows what this word *Belief* really means. Once you correct your understanding of this word, you'll transform your life for the better. This book has been specifically designed so that you can weaken the destructive

power that *beliefs* tend to exercise over a person's body, thinking processes, and nervous system.

2. The one thing you must start doing right now to triple your performance at school, work, and in personal relationships.

3. Find out *how* and *why* believing in yourself can destroy you. Never believe in yourself! Be careful. Both positive and negative thinking are potential killers.

4. Have you ever suffered from racial discrimination? Learn how to turn racism into the best friend you ever had!

5. Find out why a great memory is not necessary for becoming a great person.

6. Why must you reduce your dependence on teachers?

7. What kinds of textbooks can make or break you?

8. How can the practice of virtue increase your intelligence and success potential?

9. Master an ancient Oriental secret for penetrating to the nucleus of all facts and knowledge.

This book has been especially designed so that anyone will become more intelligent automatically by just reading it once. No exercises to perform! No Positive thinking! Nothing to believe!

Introduction

In 1964, my family and I left the marvelous little high school where I was teaching in Haysville, Kansas and headed west for the higher salaries, health benefits, retirement packages, and higher lifestyle that teachers enjoy in Southern California. Less than a week after I left the state, I had already landed a job in a California high school.

Like so many people who have never lived in California, I envisioned the state as being filled only with the most highly superior and enlightened citizens in the American union. Reality hit me in the face as if I had walked headlong into an oncoming freight train. Unlike my mostly economically and socially underprivileged students back at Campus High School in Haysville, who generally conducted themselves admirably and exhibited high standards of scholarship, their lower middle class and below California peers in the city where I went to teach, the majority of the students in the district where I was to work for the next 27 years, had little or no regard for intellectual pursuits and achievement.

After a few years in that school, I intuited correctly that I would never be able to achieve greatness as a teacher under such miserable working conditions. And, alas, as many of the colleagues who knew me at that school will be more than happy to tell you, I did not discover a way to make someone want to study and improve himself or convince him to voluntarily keep his mouth shut. *(Psst! Don't let my detractors know I told you this: Neither did they!)* However, I welcomed the opportunity to spend the years I was there, finding out the real reasons dividing high achievers and low achievers sincerely wanting to improve themselves. The goal: to find out what prevents 95 percent of all human beings from enjoying the benefits of intellectual superiority and achievement. The question: What can be done to help people break out from the mental bonds keeping their noses mashed into the mire?

After about five years of battling with those students, I suddenly realized why, other than low motivation, most people voluntarily choose to be mentally inferior the rest of their lives. I can immodestly state that I developed an amazingly effective solution to a problem that has hounded mankind ever since he quit being an ape. Seeing money possibilities in my discovery, I hurriedly wrote and published a small booklet teaching people how to enhance their intelligence. After investing a few dollars in some ten word ads in general magazines, I started earning extra money right away—not a huge fortune—but enough to finance summer-long vacations in Acapulco and Mazatlán, including occasional visits to Las Vegas.

The strong success of that little booklet, in spite of its unattractiveness, caused me to think that my message was too important to mention in so few pages. I then rewrote it, going into greater detail and giving my readers more explicit instructions on how to rid themselves of the mortal sin of stupidity and ignorance.

I don't know what held me back from telling all I had learned about I.Q enhancement: the innate human desire to fail, or modesty and incredulity that "little old me" had stumbled upon an important mental breakthrough. It was then that I put my self-doubts aside and rewrote the booklet for the third time, naming it *You Can Triple Your Intelligence!*

You Can Triple Your Intelligence! went through so many printings that I lost count. When I retired from the teaching profession in the summer of 1988, my wife and I moved up to the California High Desert. Like most recent retirees, I wanted to be free of responsibilities. At first, I tried to interest a publisher in this book, but hard, tearful experience proved to me that publishers did not share my confidence in it, regardless of the success I had enjoyed. Wanting to have free time to travel in Mexico and do research on my other pet areas of interest: the India origins of the Jews, the Old World origins of our Native-Americans, the role that the ancient Hindus played in world history and affairs, and the mystery of the Southwestern USA *Quivira* myth, I suspended publication of the book altogether.

I have since written and gotten published several books and online articles dealing with my principal areas of interest.

One day, I received an E-Mail from a certain African-American man who had read my articles and books. He asked me whether I was the Gene D. Matlock who had written *You Can Triple Your Intelligence!* I answered in the affirmative.

He told me that he had used the information in my manual to free himself of the ghetto mentality, becoming a high achiever with a key position in a major company. He also told me that a certain mail order company had pirated my book without even changing my name, continuing to sell the book successfully after I had ceased publication.

My wife advised me to sue the owner of this company. I answered, "Not on your life! This gentleman has kept my name before the public for over eleven years. Also, the letter from that reader has made me realize that it improved the lives of many people, keeping them from being sucked down the drainpipe of failure and defeat. Since giving up the publication and marketing of that book, I have discovered even better methods of increasing its effectiveness. I'm going to rewrite and update it, making it more effective and meaningful than ever before!"

Not only will this method enable any persistent, normal person to break out of his mental shackles, he will simultaneously be able to more effectively solve many of his health, economic, and social problems as well. If Society as a whole just took what I state about the tyranny of beliefs seriously, not only would mankind improve collectively, but wars and serious tensions between nations and groups could all but disappear!

In the course of your life and struggle to find self-fulfillment, you have and will come upon many mind development methods and techniques. As a seeker, you may have already tried every known theory on self-development and given up in disgust and defeat. You may even do the same with this book occasionally. But one thing I do know for sure: No matter what method you try and discard in disappointment, this manual will be the only one you'll dig out of the trashcan. Sooner or later, you'll come to realize that this book, like it or not, want it or not, can help people increase their natural level of intelligence dramatically.

If you're ready for success, why not start here?

Chapter I

Why You Should Become More Intelligent

Note: There are no exercises to perform in conjunction with this book. It is specifically designed so that the reader will automatically become more intelligent after reading it only once. Basically, the object of this book is just to make people aware of the DICTIONARY MEANING of the word "Belief". Don't allow yourself to become bored and irritated with the negative comments you'll generally find in parentheses after I mention the "B" word, which is potentially the filthiest and most dangerous word in this or any other language. In fact, the "F" word may be better than the "B" word. You will become more intelligent if and only if you realize this word's potential for destroying people and nations, both individually and collectively.

You, I, and everybody else on earth have entered one of the greatest and most frightening periods in human history—a new and, for some, a hellish level of the Industrial Revolution—The Age of Mind. In this New Age, prejudices against race, creed, sex, physical appearance, and the like will largely disappear. All humans will be divided into two castes: the elite educated and the socially undesirable ignoramuses; the knowers and the know-nothings; the skilled and the unskilled. No law on earth will be able to protect the ignoramuses adequately. They'll always qualify only for the scraps falling from the tables of the privileged intellectual elite.

In a syndicated commentary published in California newspapers on August 14, 2001, writer Dan Walters of the *Sacramento Bee* wrote:

> University of California, Davis, economist Phillip Martin and Washington-based sociologist Leon Bouvier concluded in 1985 that with the state's population expanding dramatically due to immigration, and its economy shifting from old-style manufacturing to high-technology and services, seeds were being sown for socio-economic fragmentation.
>
> 'The large increases projected for Hispanics and Asians in the labor force suggest a continuation of the emerging two-tiered economy,' Martin and Bouvier wrote in a research paper published by the Population Reference bureau, 'with Asians and better-educated non-Hispanic whites and blacks competing for the prestigious occupations while poorly educated Hispanics and blacks scramble for the lower status jobs.'
>
> If anything, they were too conservative.
>
> Socioeconomic change happened much more dramatically and more quickly…
>
> …The results directly underscore what Bouvier and Martin concluded in 1985 was beginning to happen in California.
>
> California could continue to ignore the widening socioeconomic gap or it could swallow its collective pride, acknowledge that egalitarian political rhetoric is a myth and start refocusing public resources.

It could, for instance, beef up schooling for poor-performing students, even at the cost of tilting away from college-bound suburban kids.

It could stop treating the community college system like a poor stepchild, and it could restore the vocational classes that have been widely eliminated in favor of college-prep classes...*(New Data Reveals Details of California's Two-Tier Society.)*

For some reason, Mr. Walters failed to write that unprepared Whites will also be scrounging at the bottom of the barrel with the rest of the losers in this New Age.

This New Age will turn philosophies like Communism, Capitalism, and every other "ism" into dinosaurs. The ideas of economics theoreticians like Karl Marx, Thorstein Veblen, Major Douglas, Lord Keynes, Frederick Engels, and others will become the blabbering of fools. The last time something of this magnitude happened, when the Machine Age was born, the craftsmen were brought to their knees. They had to turn wheels, twist knobs, push buttons, and oil gears or starve to death. This New Age is turning those jobs over to computer-robots. It will even deprive agricultural workers of their jobs because machines will be designed to plant and pick our crops much more rapidly, efficiently, and cheaply than hand labor.

This New Age will be less than fun for the uneducated and unprepared—heartless; unforgiving; uncompromising. Just as jungle law says, "Kill or be killed," the primary law of the Age of Mind snarls, "Educate yourself or die!" Until mankind adjusts to this new society, millions of uneducated people will experience this world as the worst conceivable sort of nightmare. Are you educated, prepared, and skilled enough to storm proof yourself against the coming hurricane? If not, you need this book, just as a person dying of thirst needs water.

Because the educational levels of most Americans have not risen to the present challenge, millions of new immigrants from other nations are turning the native-born residents of this country into the "New Indians."

In his eye-opening book *The Eco-Spasm Report,* author and futurist Alvin Toffler wrote, "...I have argued here and elsewhere that one of the really big changes of our time is a profound and rapid shift toward social and cultural diversity in the industrial nations. This splintering of once homogenous industrial societies both reflects and affects division of labor.

"Ever since Adam Smith, economists have sworn that it is highly efficient to specialize because, as Paul Samuelson's classic textbook puts it, it is 'better for fat men to do the fishing, lean men the hunting, and smart men to make the medicine...' Industrial societies have carried the division of labor to mind-staggering proportions, and any complaints about its adverse effects are usually focused on the alienation it produces in the worker. Thus Samuelson says, 'Specialization may involve some costs, breeding half men, anemic clerks, brutish stokers— and producing social alienation.' Such human costs are quickly brushed aside because, it is held, the overall efficiency of the system is radically improved...Advancing technology requires more labor division; this, in turn, fosters variety in the population...the rapid increase in the diversity of material goods and services also reflects the actual shift of the system to much higher levels of social and cultural diversity, the breakup of the homogenous industrial mass..."

At the time I first read Toffler's book, which was published in the 1980s, I, too, agreed totally that American society was becoming more and more culturally diverse in order to use the services of ethnicities specializing in certain types of labor, such as Filipino hospital laborers and Mexican strawberry pickers. But since then, the non-stop evolution of computers is proving that machines can become better fishermen, hunters, stokers, strawberry pickers, medicine manufacturers and "what-not" than humans. To find the persons educated and talented enough to design, produce and operate these machines, our industrialists are not fussy about one's race or nationality; only about his technological skills. Until now, they have not been able to find enough native-born specialists to keep scientific technology and industrial expansion abreast of the times.

How in the hell did we get in this fix?

Blame everything on middle-class fat-headedness, soft living, TV, low value systems, cowardice, weakening of the work ethic, or on the real villain—*yourself!* Like it or not, accept it or not, the native Whites, Blacks, and Browns of America, who made every sacrifice and fought every battle for peace, freedom, social equality, abundance, and progress, are acting old and feeble. They remind me of the ancient Romans who "burned out" after conquering the known world. They got so fat, middle class, lazy, and sassy that they even forced their own slaves to govern them and run their vast empire. Now, History appears to be repeating itself here. The great American industries and enterprises can no longer depend on us for the education, know-how, and sweat-and-strain to keep this country great. Therefore, more and more of us are getting fired and replaced by foreigners who aren't afraid to work and improve themselves.

Little by little we're being dumped into the sewer. *We're becoming the new "Indians."*

Now, now! Don't be so angry with old "massa!" He isn't really being unfair. Put yourself in his place. What would you do if you had millions of dollars invested in an industry, and your ungrateful, lazy workers wouldn't give you a decent day's work or turn out superior products? Would you fire them and hire responsible individuals who want to help keep your business alive and well, or would you be a "good American" and let your workers suck you down into the cesspool with them?

You must surely know that your troubles are of your own making. Back in your schooldays, weren't you one of the gang who told the teacher he wasn't making his course "fun" enough? That he should throw all the rote drills and repetitive exercises in the waste basket and teach by means of "exciting games?" Wasn't it funny to watch those unhappy teachers become frustrated when they tried to invent or find "fun" games that everyone could enjoy collectively? In my case, I was both frustrated and repentant for having entered the teaching profession. For me, study *was and is* a "fun game!"

You, as well as teachers, knew that some people prefer football; others checkers; others wrestling or boxing; some want to play cards for "fun." Not everybody likes to play the same games.

Wasn't it rib-splittingly hilarious when the muscular apes on the football team looked down at a teacher and said, "You don't have what it takes to make me want to study?" Or how about the light-hearted teachers who wanted to smile and joke instead of growling and frowning constantly? Didn't you tell them they weren't serious-minded and strict enough? That they weren't acting like "teachers?" Why didn't you look at yourself in the mirror, to find out who wasn't serious-minded and strict enough? Why didn't you act like a student? Why didn't you have your nose poked between the pages of your textbook? The teacher had his or her college degrees. Where were yours?

Did you notice that the really motivated American kids and the Asian immigrants in class didn't like for you to insult, mock, and browbeat teachers; that they didn't want any of your silly fun and games? Did you notice that all they wanted was for you to shut your yap, turn off your boom box, and get to work as they wanted to do? Sure you did!

Perhaps you have noticed that most of the schools you ever attended, and that includes the universities, always idolized "knuckle-headism" over brain power. Isn't it true that everyone was taught to respect, worship, and idolize the athletes? Back in high school, before every sporting event, we had to go to the auditorium or gymnasium and scream our heads off for the team. Those students who refused to worship them, of whom I was one, got punished for our lack of enthusiasm. I'll never forget our gym teacher and athletic director in the El Dorado, Kansas high school where I got my diploma in *nothing*. During the "pep" assemblies, Mr. McDonald would slap me on the head and scream, "Cheer for your team!" Yet, I never did in all my life attend an assembly to idolize the brainier students. It was—and still is—considered fashionable and even "politically correct"—to mock and belittle them. We like to call them "geeks" and "nerds." We like to portray them in the movies as physically underdeveloped, bumbling idiots!

Those who preferred to study when you were in high school—the ones who don't need this book—surely remember that the guys they were pressured and bullied to cheer for at pep rallies were the same gorillas who treated them like dirt. *No one ever expected them to like or respect anyone who used his mind!*

Later on, after graduation from school, we all start asking ourselves: "Why aren't the football stars who never became professional athletes as successful off the football field as on it? Why are the "geeks" and "nerds" the ones who get the best jobs, the classiest girls, and the highest salaries in the 'real world'?"

Don't tell me you don't know why!

What can we do to stop this madness?

Freedom, abundance, and progress belong only to those who are educated, honest, loyal, aware, and willing to work. From now on, a well-prepared person can be White, Black, Yellow, male, female, dwarfish, ugly, Catholic, Buddhist, fat, skinny, or whatever. It's what he has in his head cavity that counts!

We're being peed into the urinal because we're not presently educated, intelligent, honest, moral, and organized enough to keep our masters from treating us like sheep. We're being plopped into the toilet stool because we'd rather read the sports pages and watch athletic events on TV than find out what's being presented on *The Learning Channel*. I want my readers in this and any other country to know that intelligent people don't become slaves. Intelligent people don't voluntarily cut their own throats. Intelligent people don't destroy their own country.

We're all too stupid and pigheaded. Let's become more intelligent and better educated. Then and only then, will our leaders and masters, who are not really so evil as you think, bend to our collective will. Know true freedom. Save yourself, your family, your country, and your world by unchaining the giant in your own being.

Chapter II

The Prerequisite Steps to Greatness!

If you have understood this book so far, you already have all the intelligence you need. *You are already a genius!* In my three decades of teaching, I met only a dozen or so students lacking in sufficient gray matter. In theory and fact, you are already so intelligent that you will automatically be able to demonstrate your increased mind power publicly and privately by just reading this book once! There are no exercises at all to perform.

On the surface, the revelations in this chapter will appear too common and lengthy for those wanting to escape from their mental dungeons in a hurry. So, what would happen if you skipped this chapter, beginning immediately with the methods I recommend? How would it feel to "feel intelligent?" Would your life really improve? Probably not. I guarantee that you would go on feeling and acting more or less as you do now. I have told you that if you can understand this book, you have all the intelligence you need. Yet, you bought it simply because you don't feel intelligent enough. Unfortunately, not even geniuses "feel" intelligent "enough". Nobody does. You see, the mind is always aware of infinity. It knows there is always another hill to climb; another shuck hiding the goodness of an ear of corn; that it is always a few degrees below paradise. This subconscious awareness of infinity makes all humans feel inwardly dissatisfied and inadequate.

The mind is like the poor woodcutter's wife portrayed in one of my old grade school books. The woodcutter once laid down his axe, long enough to go fishing in a lake. He caught a magic fish that offered him anything he could wish for in exchange for its freedom. The man requested a better home and more abundant food; the fish complied. Later, the wife told her husband that she wanted a larger house and more luxuries. The man returned to the lake and asked the fish to increase his wealth. Again, the fish met the woodcutter's demands. The wife kept demanding more and more; the fish kept on delivering. Finally, the woman told the husband that she wanted everything in the universe. This wish the fish couldn't grant, for the universe is always expanding in eternal time and space. Therefore, it reduced the couple to their former condition of poverty.

The story teaches us to never stop appreciating, counting, and using the blessings we already possess. A person who can't be happy where he is will feel no happier or more intelligent anywhere else, for wherefore a person finds himself, either higher or lower, rich or poor, there he *is*. This I say to you now: You have at this moment all the gray matter and intelligence you need to do or become anything. All you need are the right tools and attitudes to demonstrate your natural superiority.

First and foremost, face the truth that your worst enemy is your own laziness and pigheadedness. Have you ever wondered why so many people buy and read books on magic, witchcraft, and psychic development? You probably bought this book, hoping that I would show you a magic no-work way to become what I know you already are. Too many of us want things to come easily. Naturally, we'll lend a ready ear to those who assure us that all we have to do is kneel before a few lighted candles and utter some absurd chants. A person yearning for psychic awareness is not honest enough to admit that he really wants to choose winning horses without first learning all he can about the horses and their jockeys. I used to be such a fool. I used to be a sucker for "psychic awareness" methods and fads. A popular Buddhist sect here in California hooks suckers by promising that their "magic chant," along with fanatical participation in the sect, will help them become or do anything. Just two years after I swallowed their bait, I was able to inflate a 300 dollars inheritance to a sixty-five thousand dollars a year business. But one day, I began to wonder why my need for money was being satisfied while some other pressing needs and problems kept worsening with every chant I uttered. My leaders told me that my "bad karma" was the "why." Some "born-again" Christians whispered that the Devil and his little demons were pushing my sudden financial success. However, what sanity I had left told me that I was working hard and confidently to amass wealth and doing little or nothing to solve the other problems plaguing my existence. The "Devil" of which my "born-again" stalkers were so terrified was in reality the establishment of goals and the guts to reach them. When I realized that "God-helps-those-who-help-themselves" is probably the only magic chant that works, I freed myself of gurus, "psychics," and most superstitions forever. I now never let myself forget, not even for a moment, that Nature showers miracles only on those who are willing to help themselves. If you ever find yourself drowning in a river and expect a miracle or blind belief in your favorite deity to take you to shore, you'll end up at the bottom of that river. Nature (the real word for God), will reveal its reality to you only in your willingness to paddle to shore. This chapter will show you how to become a person who helps himself.

Step I
Free yourself from Dependence on Teachers.

One of my ex-high school students, now a successful businessman, once told me, "I want you and all the other teachers at the high school to know that you didn't teach me anything. Everything I got in life I got on my own."

"Tony," I answered, "You and I have a lot in common. No teacher ever taught me anything, either."

I first realized that teaching is a myth after taking a high school Spanish class. I took to Spanish as a duck takes to water. I adored and revered my Spanish teacher, as I still do (may she rest in peace), because of her "skills in imparting foreign language skills to a clout like me. She made the study so easy. I said to myself at the time, "I'll not rest until I know as much Spanish as she does." After finishing that first year class, my passion for Spanish led me to Mexico where I entered a Mexican college, becoming fluent in the language. After achieving fluency, I returned to her class to speak to her in Spanish at "her level." I discovered that she couldn't even say "¡Sí!" I also discovered that she knew not one jot or tittle about Spanish grammar and pronunciation. She must have been like a certain high school principal who once bragged to me, "I have never studied Spanish; neither can I read, write, speak or understand it. But I can teach it."

After surviving the traumatic realization that my beloved Spanish teacher didn't know her subject matter, I realized that I had just tricked myself into believing *(regarding unproven ideas as gospel)* she was using "superior teaching methods" or some fun form of magic to squirt Spanish grammar into my brain. The truth was that as her student, I had given her credit for what I was accomplishing totally on my own. A statement she made to me should furnish extra proof that no one really "teaches." "Gene, in all my forty years of teaching Spanish, you are the only one of my students to learn it."

The absurdity *(a satisfactory definition of most beliefs)* that only God, teachers, or magic can make people learn came into vogue several millenniums ago. Furthermore, ancient man believed *(lied to himself)* that "God" permitted only a chosen few to master even such mundane subjects as reading, writing, and mathematics. Early man also believed *(imagined)* that teachers were magicians directly appointed by God to impart knowledge. He was totally convinced *(self-deluded)* that without teachers, the magician-emissaries of God, possessors of divine, supernatural powers, nobody could learn or progress. Anyone wanting the "keys to the universe" often wasted most of his life seeking the right "con artist" capable of convincing him that he, too, could learn. Even today, spiritual seekers, especially of the California variety, preserve the superstition that they can find the Way only by blindly obeying the mind vomit of their self-styled gurus. This blind adoration of gurus originated in India; it is called **Guru-Kula.**

My experiences as a teacher showed me that the worst and laziest students believe *(make themselves more stupid than ever before)* that unskilled or too lenient teachers are the cause of their cloutishness. A typical comment teachers got and get from them is, "I ain't good in school 'cuz my teachers don't know how to teach me right and make learnin' fun enough." Yet, the good students work far more independently and require much less discipline than the clouts and oafs. We need discipline in classrooms so that the dummies and clowns, who shouldn't be there anyway, won't bother those who do want to learn. People wonder why Asian children are generally good students. Having had them in my classes, I know that most of them take total responsibility for their successes and failures, whereas the non-Asian students generally will not. One of my friends, who was transferred from an inner city school to a predominantly Filipino school in Artesia, California, told me happily, "I have died and gone to Heaven!"

If you are one of those who believe *(the favorite verb of those who accept nonsense as demonstrable evidence)* that teachers must pull you around by the nose and kick your butt, you will never get anywhere until you realize that you, and only you, are your only teacher and savior! Never be a sheep. Sheep need shepherds.

Step II
Become a Do-it-Yourself Foreigner!

Grow up now! Take responsibility for yourself! Don't blame your stupidity and failures on your teachers, leaders, parents, social class, race, culture, religion, age, or environment. For too long, you have probably been demanding that your teachers and leaders become "foreigners" and provide you with the entertainment, services, and goods that you are too hateful, lazy and shiftless to get for yourself. Instead, wave your "magic wand" and turn yourself into a *do-it-yourself foreigner* who starts from nothing; who without any encouragement or financial help from anyone rolls up his sleeves, gets his hands dirty, and fights his way to the stars against every obstacle. Defecate addiction to fun and games from your soul. Kick that lousy habit once and for all! Let your struggle be your fun. Make learning a sport.

Of course, regardless of what I say, you may still insist on some kind of "fun-and-games" way to jumpstart yourself. If your teachers won't give your class any "fun learning games", here's a great solitaire game you can play all by yourself: **If you study and work hard, you win. If you waste your life, you lose!**

Don't fret about the boring, no-fun aspects of learning, working, saving, and achieving. There's nothing wrong with boredom or boring people. Boredom is the kick in the butt people need to make something of their lives. The foreigners who come here to do your thinking and empty your bedpans didn't have much fun in school or at home, back in their native lands. They didn't know how to be bored because they were too poor to enjoy such a luxury back in the "Old Country." Believe *(become a fool)* it or not, my Asian students were among the few who didn't cry for fun-n'-games teaching strategies. They knew that they'd have fun later, once they got educated enough to push lazy, silly American Johnny aside and take the absorbing, fascinating, high-paying jobs offered to those with knowledge, intelligence, patience, and the will to work.

I once heard a young woman advise her friends never to have a boyfriend who loved libraries and studying. She told them, "Such boys don't know the least thing about sex!" She didn't know how far afield she was. When I was a teenager, I searched for my lovers in the libraries. I knew that through their studies, they had probably discovered a few tidbits of sexual wisdom that could help a young man feel perky.

Step III
Give as well as take.

Always go that extra mile—at work—at play—in your family and social relationships. Show everyone that you give as well as take. On your job, work overtime as often as possible—without pay! The person who wants instant gratification whenever he bats his eyes is thinking only of the here-and-now. He's not acting like a *foreigner!* The person giving his boss a few extra well-worked hours a week becomes a "do-it-yourself foreigner" who gets many delayed action bonus-bombs consisting of raises, promotions, job security, recognition, and other blessings. He will ultimately strike it rich at the top of the heap where the rewards are greater.

Step IV
The Basic Skills Opening the Doors of the Mind.

One of the greatest and most effective brain development methods known to man is just the study of vocabulary. The simple, unglamorous truth: The more words you learn and use, the more intelligent you become. The fewer words you know and use, the more stupid you are. Armed with a large vocabulary, your mind can understand, interpret, apply, and develop a wider variety of ideas and thoughts. A good vocabulary is as close as any paperback dictionary. Memorize and use every word. If you prefer self-teaching textbooks on this subject, the average bookstore can serve you well. Don't forget: *While you're developing your vocabulary, be sure to learn the difference between the words BELIEVE, NOT-BELIEVE, KNOW, and NOT-KNOW!* A correct knowledge of these two words alone will rocket your mind to the stars.

Step "Anything."

The immortal mathematician-philosopher Alfred North Whitehead wrote, "…Civilization advances by extending the number of operations which we can perform without thinking about them." Don't forget the above statement. It harbors even the secret of ending all wars and group conflicts forever.

Whitehead was discussing the importance of overlearning in education. All the basic, necessary skills for living successfully should be drilled into the student so often that he will be able to recall them automatically and effortlessly for the rest of his life.

I am reminded of the tale of an old man who had a knee-length beard. One day, his grandson asked him, "Grampa, when you retire at night, do you tuck your beard under the blankets, or do you let it lie on top of them?"

The old man replied, "I have never thought about that. I will watch carefully what I do tonight and give you my answer tomorrow." That night, he crawled into bed and laid the beard out neatly on top of the blankets. However, when turning to the right or to the left, he felt as if the beard would be jerked out by the roots. The pain was intolerable. When he put his beard under the blankets, the whiskers scratched at his chest, causing a mind-shaking itching. In order to get some rest that night, the poor fellow had to get up and shave off his luxuriant, beloved beard.

By "overlearning" material, you can increase your mental efficiency tenfold. Not thinking about the variables and operations involved in grammar, writing, and mathematics will leave your mind open to greater creativity in your chosen field.

Here are the basic instructions for overlearning: Master a chapter in the text you are studying. Study it again, going over every detail; answer every question in the quizzes. Afterwards, go to the next lesson, reviewing the previous lesson in your spare time. It will also profit you to rewrite the chapter in your own words, pretending that you are trying to make the course understandable to people of a lower educational level.

Do not put time limits on yourself. One of the greatest barriers to getting educated is the old-fashion system of grade levels: in first grade, this; in second grade, that, etc. In college, a certain history course may be unrealistically designed to last a semester. You may need more than a semester. Therefore, the "system" punishes you by giving you an "F" for not being able to finish the race at the same time the brainier students do. This state of affairs must stop—now! Give yourself all the time you need to learn a subject. Some people will be able to learn a certain course in a week. Others may need a year. A few may need all the lives to do it. Who cares? Keep plodding until you see light at the end of the tunnel!

At age 32, hen I was working in my father's real estate business, he told me to devote more time to the business and less to traveling and enjoying myself—or get out. I chose to leave the business.

Here's the way I looked at old "Father Time" when Dad kicked me out of his business. I said to myself, "I can get a job right now and work for less than desirable wages, working conditions, and two week vacations for the rest of my life. I can also choose to spend the next two years getting my Master's Degree and become a foreign language teacher. Although salaries of professional teachers may not be the best, the obligation-free summers they do receive are enviable. I can use this free time to roast myself to a golden brown on the beaches of Acapulco, Mazatlán, and other delightful Mexican beach resorts from two to three months a year."

I chose to suffer for two years and become a teacher. Although I came to hate being a classroom teacher working under the deplorable conditions that many Southern California teachers suffered at the time, I loved the summer vacations. My wife and I even spent our Christmases in Mazatlán and Las Vegas! At least one weekend a month, we enjoyed ourselves in Tijuana.

It's O.K. to speed up the learning process whenever this is possible. Needless to say, large, meaty textbooks are inappropriate for the over-learner. Bulky, porky textbooks are too lardy to be overlearned; they also stifle most people's ambition to get educated. All textbooks should be made as skinny as is humanly possible, presenting only the material to be overlearned. Most teachers fear that such basic textbooks prevent students from getting "insights," but just the reverse is true in nearly all cases. The analysis-prone human mind is amazingly capable of observing a sequence of events, combinations, or conditions and of arriving at its own conclusions. Schools, teachers, courses, and texts should conform to the old maxim for political speakers: "If you must be dull, at least have the good sense to be brief."

I had a friend in Mexico who was an expert linguist, musician, grammarian, mathematician, and civil engineer. Though he was born in poverty in Mexico City's squalid *Tepito* market place, known also as "Thieves Market," though he never attended any school or received any diploma, even the titled experts consulted him on his specialties—bridge construction and building demolition.

How did he acquire his impressive collection of knowledge? By mastering fat, blubbery textbooks? Not on your life! Had he chose the mountain-sized textbook route to freedom, he would probably still be an illiterate, jobless Indian selling tacos on the street. He just discovered what any successful learner knows: the average textbook is just a jungle of words and boring explanations designed, on purpose, to discourage would-be geniuses. In his classic self-teaching calculus text, a book selling briskly for nearly one hundred years at this date, author Silvanus P. Thompson wrote, "Considering how many fools can calculate, it is surprising that it should be thought either a difficult or a tedious task for any other fool to learn how to master the same tricks…The fools who write the textbooks of advanced mathematics—and they are mostly clever fools—seldom take the trouble to show you how easy the easy calculations are. On the contrary, they seem to desire to impress you with their tremendous cleverness by going about it in the most difficult way."

The people wanting you to keep on thinking small don't want you to wake up as my Mexican friend did. That's why they make textbooks intentionally theoretical and bulky. That's why they hire "teachers" to make sure that only a chosen few will find the needles in those haystacks called "classroom textbooks." In this way, they can keep the demand for their highly-paid specialties free of competition.

I will go so far as to declare that "overlearning," far from being the bane of students, is one of the fastest ways to become a genius. When I was in the Marine Corps during the Korean War, our sergeant made us field strip and reassemble our M-1 rifles until we could do it blindfolded. When I could do it perfectly, I then concentrated on speed. After I was able to field-strip the weapon and put it back together in a few seconds, I concentrated on cleaning and oiling the weapon blindfolded after I had field-stripped it. When I was able to field strip, clean, and oil it, reassembling it with lightning speed, I then concentrated on field stripping and reassembling every part by barely touching it. I did this as a hobby. By time I was discharged, I probably knew more about the M-1 blindfolded than the inventor did with his eyes wide open. Without realizing it, I had stumbled upon an ancient Oriental secret for penetrating to the nucleus of all facts and knowledge: *overlearning*, or the practice of repeating and extending awareness of facts and knowledge far, far beyond the amount of repetition and time needed to remember and understand them well. An example of overlearned facts are the multiplication tables. To over-learn something, you must repeat it over, over, and over again by rote, as I continue to emphasize. Yes, rote learning is the whipping dog of both educators and learners. Even so, it is one of the shortest and best possible routes that anyone can take to attain genius in his specialty.

Hoping that I have thus far convinced you that overlearning and extending your awareness of something you've overlearned are blessings, not curses, I'm now going to give you an assignment that will take the rest of your life. Choose a subject or a field that interests you. It does not have to be broad. Make it your passion in life. Don't go to bed at night until you have found at least a tiny molecule of something new. Remember: you don't have to choose a broad subject. Just keep on penetrating it ever more deeply, vowing never even to rest until you learn something new every day. As your knowledge gets deeper and deeper—more and more extensive—people will gasp in awe at your knowledge of this subject. They'll start calling you a *genius*!

I also want to add that in order to learn all you can of a certain subject, you may even have to master other disciplines. Therefore, narrowing down to a specialty won't necessarily make you narrow-minded regarding this subject. Master any other subject that will increase your depth in your field of specialty.

Many so-called "authorities" stupidly say that rote learning and overlearning destroy creativity, making people react like parrots or robots. Just the reverse is true as I proved to myself with the M-1 exercises.

Do you need a fabulous memory?

Nearly everyone would like to have a photographic memory. They associate a photographic memory with genius. However, some idiot savants have photographic memories. Many geniuses are as famous for being forgetful as they are for being geniuses. Have you ever heard of the absent-minded professor? It isn't necessary for you to have more than an average memory in order to learn effectively. Also, just the rote-learning alone will lead you to mastery of subjects.

There are a number of fine memory courses on the market, but most people grow weary of and bored with them. Memory showmen use special systems which must be thoroughly mastered before one can perform mental tricks. Just keeping those systems in one's mind all the time can drive a person wacky. I advise students not to worry too much about their memories. Instead, they should concentrate on overlearning the course material. However, the following advice will help you retain better without having to master complicated and really boring memory courses.

The subconscious mind receives facts from the conscious mind and then catalogues them in categories and associations. It organizes these categories and associations with the material already in its files, which it organized with previous input from the conscious mind. Then, when the conscious mind wants to recall certain facts, the subconscious searches through its files, extracts the facts requested, and sends them back to the conscious mind. It just stands to reason that the more ignorant and uneducated a person is, the fewer file classifications will he have stored in his subconscious memory banks. Therefore, the more learning experiences a person acquires, either through actual hands-on experience or through written words, etc., the more easily can he memorize, understand, and apply facts.

The subconscious mind must take some time to decide just where to file input or to find where it has been filed and bring it out again. Its task is often made more difficult by input signals of tension, fear, and worry from the conscious mind. Under these poor conditions, and with no direction from its conscious "computer operator," the subconscious mind may need several days or more to catalogue and associate input and then process it back to the conscious mind (memory). If you will save your conscious mind the task of and time needed for filing input by telling it from the beginning just where and how the input is to be filed, catalogued, and associated, you'll memorize faster, more efficiently, and more easily.

Convert all individual, series, and combinations of facts, objects, skills, and words to vivid mind-picture associations. These associations need not make sense. Man first thought with his feelings and mind's eye before refashioning images into words. These associations, categories, and comparisons must have a life of their own. They can and must be made dramatic and meaningful through different rhythms, sounds, colors, movements, smells, etc. Exaggerate their size, form and qualities—or minimize them. Make big things small and inoffensive; make small things large and intimidating. Imagine them as being out of proportion, comical, sexy, scary, nasty, and even vulgar. House them with, stick them in, or poise them under, beside, or over equally exaggerated or compressed things, either related or unrelated. For example, picture a thumb-size, squeaking elephant fleeing from a trumpeting elephant-size mouse.

Here's how I remembered the name of a man named Michael Wishnak: I pictured him as Mickey (Mouse), down on his knees, palms pressed together in humble supplication, pleading, begging, and desperately wishing for a snack!

It's neither necessary nor important for people to memorize every bit of information with which they come in contact. Albert Einstein didn't mind not knowing how many feet are in a mile. Furthermore, he didn't want to know! But he did want to remember everything possible about his specialty: pure mathematics. You, too, should emulate Einstein, adopting the philosophy that it's not a sin to forget certain things. Why clutter your memory with trivia? However, like Einstein, you should memorize perfectly the facts you need to grow personally and professionally in your chosen area. I also advise you to become fanatical about memorizing the faces, names, and details of almost every person you meet. People feel unusually honored and complimented when strangers and acquaintances take the time and effort to engrave their names, physical characteristics, and other pertinent data in their mental history books. They reward their "ego boosters' with popularity and an open path up the ladder of success.

When you meet a person, review his name and other physical and personal data several times while you are still in his presence. Try to associate and link peculiarities of his name and physical features. To remember a man named Joe Thatcher, I glanced at his unkempt hair and said to myself several times, "Joe Thatcher's head sho' looks like he thatched'er!" To remember the name of an ex-student named Virginia

Palmerin, who had no strange physical characteristics, I pictured her as a virgin with a palm tree growing out of the top of her head.

You should also keep a written notebook containing important and even trivial facts about the customers, professional and work associates, and other individuals who can contribute to your overall growth. Review your notes at every opportunity. You may also want to convert your notes to flashcards.

Hard work, grammar, mathematics, geometry, virtuous conduct, and worldly wisdom are keys to total mental liberation!

If you overlearned the bare bones of grammar, practical mathematics, and geometry to the point where you could express yourself in those subjects subconsciously, you would indeed triple your intelligence!

How does grammar study increase intelligence? It prepares people to put their large vocabulary to work in an orderly, effective fashion. Then and only then do a person's speech and writing become weapons capable of toppling or building empires. In my opinion *(Never forget: all opinions, even mine, are just beliefs—potential mind vomit)*, only one completely effective basic grammar text has ever been written: *English 3200,* by Joseph Blumenthal, originally published by Harcourt, Brace, and World.

Eliphas Levi, the great Jewish cabalist, wrote in *El Libro de los Esplendores (The Book of Splendors)*, that mathematics and geometry "…establish…an exact classification of all human knowledge…Nothing is more ingenius, logical, and exact…the way to obtain exactly all possible deductions; to obtain new knowledge and to develop the spirit, without leaving anything to the defectiveness of the imagination…in a certain way, it forces Nature to reveal her secrets…Once the knowledge is acquired, one moves to the ultimate revelations of the transcendental

Cabala, and one studies in the *Chemanporach* the source of and the reason for all dogmas."

Geometry and mathematics are the starting points *par excellence* toward the goal of all worldly and divine knowledge. They are the father and mother of art, music, science, creativity, and achievement; the foundation stones of all order, symmetry, and truth. All things; all beings; all conditions; all ideas contain an inherent form or pattern, either seen or unseen; either known or unknown. By an exhaustive study and application of geometry alone, all the other truths will ultimately flower, including the highest levels and quality of intelligence. A person who has mastered formal geometry learns how to discern truth and untruth with almost superhuman exactness. He can apply his skills to penetrate to the heart of both mathematical and non-mathematical subjects.

Unfortunately for the future of most people in the world, only a few people have an adequate knowledge of mathematics and geometry. Fifty percent of Americans are barely able to add their grocery bills. I myself did not master basic mathematics until my early 20s. God only knows how I was able to get through college with only a fourth grade equivalent of mathematical skills. Believe *(Become a fool)* it or not, one of my enemies rescued me. While a college student in Mexico, and after a previous love affair in that country, I established formal relations with another beautiful girl. Her brother-in-law, one of Mexico's leading artists, hated Americans and used every means to make us look ridiculous which, in my case, was an easy goal to achieve. One day, he said to my girlfriend, "Most Americans are stupid. Moreover, I can prove it. They are so stupid that they can barely add." He then dared me to solve a simple problem involving the division of fractions. I failed it miserably. So distressed was I for having made my countrymen look bad, I resolve to correct my deficiencies in math. I started with a self-teaching book of arithmetic. One year later (It took me nine months to solve a certain problem in the book), I graduated to an autodidactic course in algebra. My journey through that subject was torturous. I kept a careful record of how long it took me to master (overlearn) certain topics: the powers of 10, five times; special products and factoring, 6 tries; linear equations, 5 times; special products and factoring, 6 tries; linear equations, 5 times; systems of linear equations, 8 tries; roots and radicals, 10 times; quadratic equations, 10 painful rounds before achieving success. After algebra, I attacked a do-it-yourself geometry course, leaving a trail of blood every step of the way. Trigonometry I breezed through, for regardless of the horribly fat trigonometry books on the market, purposely written that way to discourage anyone wanting to improve himself, a person can master the subject in less than a week! Just remember: the triangles used in trigonometry must be converted to algebraic expressions. Calculus, supposedly the highest form of mathematics, is no less difficult if one keeps in mind that it is nothing more than a study of slope-finding hidden behind a frightening Halloween mask and reams of scholarly writing which, I am sure, were wickedly designed to scare and discourage people wanting to compete with guys like Albert Einstein.

The elephant-size math books presently used in our public schools are bristling with word problems dealing with the solutions to physics problems, statistics, compound interest, and a host of other "practical" applications of mathematics. But what about those students who won't become physicists? How many will pass their state real estate exams and sell houses? The job of just learning how to solve math problems is great enough unto itself. Once a person learns math, he can then learn how to solve word problems. After that, he can acquire the finer points of practical applications by studying for the career of his choice. When you choose your do-it-yourself math text or computer math course, choose one that presents only a minimum of word problems.

At this point, you may feel like commenting, "Matlock must be crazy. I bought this book to find out how to get smart enough to learn mathematics, geometry, and grammar, only to find out that these subjects in themselves develop the intellect. How can I get intelligent enough to learn what I need to know to become intelligent." Well, as I keep repeating over and over in this book, you already are intelligent. In fact, you're a genius. And you can prove it right now by increasing your efforts in all areas. *Tripling your effort = Tripling your intelligence!*

The Magic Power of Virtuous Conduct.

The immortal 17th century Spanish philosopher-priest, Baltasar Gracián, perhaps the greatest authority on worldly wisdom in all the history of the Western World, wrote:

In a word, be a saint; that says everything. Virtue is a chain of all perfections, the center of all happiness. She makes you prudent, discreet, shrewd, sensible, wise, brave, cautious, honest, happy, praiseworthy, true…a universal hero. Three things make one blessed: saintliness, wisdom, and prudence. Virtue is the sun of the lesser world, and its hemisphere is a good conscience. It is so lovely that it wins God's grace and that of others. There is nothing as lovable as virtue, nor as hateful as vice. Virtue alone is for real, all else is sham. Talent and greatness depend on virtue, not on fortune. Only virtue is sufficient unto herself. She makes us love the living and remember the dead.

The Hindu philosopher-historian Kuttikhat Purushothama Chon wrote in his book, *Remedy the Frauds in Hinduism:*

Saiva faith declares that 'from virtue wealth is derived and from wealth enjoyment.' Our modern youths will readily admit that 'from wealth enjoyment is derived;' but they will laugh at the idea that 'wealth is derived from virtue.' They will say that wealth is derived from cheating and foul play only. The meaning of 'wealth derived from virtue' is too deep to understand. Let us take an example: A man acquires a lot of wealth by unholy means. The process goes on. Cheating and foul play become his way of life. Because of this, he is not respected in the society. His sons, daughters and other relations are treated with contempt in the society. With the result, his sensitive son becomes a rebel. His character and conduct land him in jail, or he becomes quite unworthy in his own home and outside. He squanders the easily earned wealth of his father. Can the father and the son enjoy that wealth they earned by foul means? (p. 335.)

In many societies, a virtuous, tender-hearted person is looked upon as a sucker—a *freier*, as the Israelis say—one who allows others to take advantage of him. But this is not necessarily so. Father Baltasar Gracián preached that virtuous people must also be shrewd. Upon reflection, it is easy to understand how and why a virtuous person can become richer and more socially prominent than one who uses corrupt means to win fortune and recognition in life. People of abundant material means and power know that they can trust such a person to help them run their enterprises and protect their wealth. If the virtuous person is an independent entrepreneur, his clients can be assured that they will be dealt with fairly and honestly.

For many people, the word "virtuous" means being a person who will not indulge in sexual relations beyond the bonds of matrimony. However, I have met a number of non-virgins in my lifetime, who in every way were paragons of virtue. The most virtuous non-virgin I ever met in my life was a Korean whore. When I was serving with the Marine Corps during the Korean conflict in the early 50s, I, as well as many other American soldiers, were fond of making regular visits to this breathtakingly beautiful Taegu prostitute whom we called "Big Tits Cutie," so-called because of her incredibly firm melon-sized breasts that jutted forward naughtily without any need of a brassiere or other support to maintain them in a near horizontal position. She was truly a marvel to behold!

"Big Tits Cutie" used all of her abundant earnings from prostitution—and from charging American soldiers wanting to photograph her sumptuous breastworks—to house, medicate, feed, clothe, and educate Korean war orphans. Not one cent of her wealth did she use to pamper herself. She sacrificed her body and her reputation for the good of those motherless children. I can think of no virtue greater than Cutie's unselfish altruism!

What is worldly wisdom?

Baltasar Gracián (1601-1658) was a famous Spanish Jesuit priest who taught that by learning how to survive successfully in this world, a person would automatically earn the reward of everlasting life after leaving the body. No one hated human foolishness more than he. He spent his life observing great people and collecting valid strategies that would help people become successful in this world. The Church did not approve of his worldliness. Although the Church never defrocked him, the ecclesiastical leaders of the time banned his works and restricted his freedom in other ways. In the final weeks of his life, he wrote:

> My health is failing. There is not much time remaining, perhaps a few months at best. Before I ascend to eternal peace, I am obliged, as all men are, to leave my contributions of earthly gratitude.

> What better way to accomplish this than to warn future generations that the art of self-preservation is at the heart of survival? Or to point out that life is an ever-constant battle, and to alert those intent upon making their fortune in the world to the hidden intentions in human behavior. The world is an illusionary place and dangers abound…

> I have dedicated my life to testimonies that needed to be heard by the populace, only to find, in the waning days, that nothing tangible remains: My voice has no listeners, my published writings are banned and have mysteriously disappeared. The bishop has decreed that anyone who did not turn in my books would be guilty of mortal sin. It is as though I never existed! But if this punishment was meant to break my will, it did not succeed.

> I often think of the days gone by and the many events that shaped my life. I think of my constant conflicts with certain leaders of the Church. Whoever said 'He has the patience of a

saint' must have had a survivor in mind, for how else does anyone prevail? (Taken from *The Wisdom of Baltasar Gracián—A Practical Manual For Good and Perilous Times;* adapted and edited by J. Leonard Kaye.)

In the preface of this book, Mr. Kaye says:

He counseled kings. His books were translated intro every language in the civilized world. The greatest minds of Europe—Friedrich Nietzsche and Arthur Schopenhauer—drew inspiration from his writings. He was considered the genius of his age, yet the name Baltasar Gracián is unknown to all but a select few…

Gracián's visionary words touch our minds and spirits, but they are not of a religious bent. Rather, his common sense material deals with men and women engaged in the business of living in a highly charged, aggressive era. His observations force us to examine our assets and our limitations. He helps us solve the many puzzles of life.

Gracián's seventeenth-century world of corruption, poverty, hypocrisy, and widespread disintegration of moral values bears a frightening resemblance to today's world. His writings constantly warn decent men that the corridors of commerce are filled with traitors and tricksters.

As in Gracián's time, today people in positions of power can be toppled by the whim of someone of higher rank. Gracián warns that we must recognize the shadows that precede these events. Business opportunities are often lost when we are outmaneuvered by clever adversaries. Anticipation is the key to circumventing back-stabbing and other personal catastrophes. In a world of conflict and crisis, honed principles of survival are compulsory for successful interaction with one another. In the end, we must win…

Following Gracián's line of thought, spiritual preparedness, and calm alertness lead to business, political, and personal power. For men and women who are maneuvering to safeguard their positions in the business world, and for others who are trying to establish them, these cerebral tools can be effective only as long as the undertow of rivalry and shrewd opposition is recognized…

Throughout, Gracián is a fascinating role model for survival. His own heroic story becomes the framework for his teachings, drawing readers into his surgical probings of life, with insights that are as applicable in today's world as they were centuries ago….

In meeting the enlightened Baltasar Gracián you may also feel the inspiration and gain the spiritual strength to walk up to a 'stone wall, paint a door on it, and walk through.'" *(xxiii-xxvi, in passim.)*

Unlike many biblical prophets and teachers, Gracián in no way taught people to be sissies. He did not urge anyone to 'turn the other cheek,' neither did his idea of being virtuous include any kind of martyrdom. For example, he recommended:

If you would lead, let others take responsibility for errors. It is the wise strategy of those who govern, in state or industry, to carry a shield against vicious ill will pledged against them. They must know how to let the responsibility for something amiss rest upon another. It is not a mark of weakness, as the envious think, but of greater strength to have on hand someone to bear the brunt for failure in order to continue to govern without hindrance. Weigh the situation at hand. It may be a wise business decision to let someone atone for your errors even though it cost you some of your pride. Self-preservation is in the heart of survival. Not everything can come off well, nor everyone be satisfied.

Do not play to lose. For some, failure is a way of life. Having started down the wrong road, they think it is a badge of character to be consistent. They admit their error to their inner selves, but to those in the outer world who will listen, they readily offer reasons and excuses that validate their actions. To this end they are marked pathetic fools, as they go about slowly starving the roots of life. They should know neither impulsive promise nor wrong resolve are bending upon any man, and yet some will on this account continue in their sulkiness, and carry on to their contrariness, as though being constant in their idiocies proves their strength of character.

Do not die of another's misery. Beware of those mired in misfortune who call to you for comfort. These men are on the hunt for those who will help them carry their baggage of adversity. You hear from them intermittently, yet they have no twinge of conscience about asking for a helping hand. Know that these men cleverly maintain relationships with the softhearted, even those whom they have bluffed and cheated in the past. Great coolness is necessary with the drowning if you would bring them help without peril to yourself.

As you can easily see, although Father Gracián was a Catholic priest, not all his teachings adhered closely to the teachings of Jesus Christ. Father Gracián taught people how to avoid crucifixion at all costs; not to experience it.

Until now, no one has ever been able to upstage the teachings of Baltasar Gracián. Had I read his books in my youth, my life would have been less rocky. To live your life more successfully, you must study his teachings carefully. I recommend the following books: *The Wisdom of Baltasar Gracián—A Practical Manual for Good and Perilous Times;* adapted and edited by J. Leonard Kaye. Published by Pocket Books, NY, and *The Art of Worldly Wisdom—a Pocket Oracle;* translated by Christopher Maurer. Published by Doubleday Dell Publishing Group, NY.

About Hard Physical Labor.

Many people have so wasted their precious lives, such as living on welfare, begging, and the like, that they are even ignorant of how to bend their backs, lift, and carry. For some of my readers, hard physical labor may be their only available starting point in beginning new lives as intelligent persons. Americans are great complainers. They especially like to rant and rave self-righteously about those "damn Mexican illegals who enter this country and take all our jobs." One of my neighbors always grumbles about "Mexicans being on welfare," but she herself has been on welfare in all the 12 years I've known her. Such Americans appear convinced that grumbling alone solves the problem of illegal aliens. They don't like to do anything to make themselves marketable as laborers. One of these days—I can't predict in which century—our P.E. teachers, who themselves desperately need to learn how to become more intelligent—will stop teaching people how to be effective basketball and football players. Instead, they will teach their students how to be effective physical laborers. When that happens, *America may go back to work!*

To not suffer too much from physically demanding jobs, the laborer must exercise and strengthen the muscles used to perform the required operations for his particular type of work. Let's use strawberry-picking as an example. Here in Southern California, people often see strawberry pickers bending over in fields beside the freeways. They say to themselves, "Poor things! They're suffering so much. How glad I am not to be a strawberry picker." I call such pity "wasted sympathy." If people knew about the high wages paid to strawberry pickers, perhaps they'd park their cars alongside the freeway and enter those fields themselves! Most people don't even believe me when I tell them what a good strawberry picker can earn in one day. I'm being modest when I say that a good strawberry picker can earn twice as much—and more—as the average working man, skilled or unskilled!

To survive in the strawberry-picking game, one must learn how to remain squatted for long periods of time. Also, he must develop all the muscles in his hands. If I wanted to become a strawberry picker, I would practice duck-walking and rolling up newspapers in my fist. Sit-ups and stand-ups from a squatting position would also help, because after picking a certain amount of strawberries, the picker then must stand up and run as fast as possible to the person who accepts and tallies his work output. One of my Mexican friends, who picked strawberries for more than 40 years before retiring, told me that when one becomes expert at this type of labor, it becomes ridiculously easy.

While working, laborers may not be able to talk or enjoy themselves as trained professionals can do. Hard labor can be made more tolerable if the worker will get with his friends at the end of the day and relax. On midday Saturday, after receiving their paychecks, the workers and their friends can also relax together while drinking some ice-cold beer, just so long as they don't overdo—if you know what I mean.

One of the dangers in being a physical laborer is that a person gets an excellent excuse not to improve himself at the end of the workday: "I'm too tired to improve myself." Perhaps such a person should move upward in slow steps, such as taking a night course in being a cashier at a convenience store.

Chapter III

The Key to Genius!

What is a genius? Does he learn more easily and faster than others? Maybe yes; maybe not. Some geniuses are slow learners; some are not; Some have excellent memories; some do not. Some wooden-heads are fast learners; some are not.

The major ingredient in the recipe for mental superiority, the one that determines who is or is not a genius, is *persistence.* A genius has the persistence and patience to stick with a problem until it is solved. Thomas A. Edison said, "Genius is one percent inspiration and ninety-nine percent perspiration." George Polye wrote in *Mathematical Discovery,* "A good problem solver must be obstinate; he must stick to his problem; he must not give up…Stick to the point examined till there is hope for some useful suggestion."

As I stated in the last chapter, I kept studying mathematics stubbornly, just like a snapping turtle, not relaxing until I had mastered what I wanted to know of something I should've mastered back in grade school. While serving with the Marine Corps in Korea, I struggled with the same problem for nine months before conquering it. My comrades-in-arms advised me to look up the answer in the back of the book and then move on to the next topic. But I knew one thing that they didn't. Each topic in mathematics is a foundation upon which the next one must be built. If I failed to solve that troublesome problem on my own, I would be constructing my knowledge of more advanced topics on a fragile foundation. I had to solve that problem satisfactorily in order to keep all that I had built up from tumbling down like the legendary walls of Jericho.

Later on in life, I began to wonder about the origins of the Jewish people. It seemed impossible that one could find the origins of a people before writing was invented. However, I kept struggling with this problem without giving up. One day, I looked in an atlas of the Ancient World, finding that a River Cophen really did exist in Afghanistan. After that, I kept searching in libraries for some hint of who Abraham and Sarah were. I found out that they were just personifications of the Hindu deities Brahm and Sara-svati. On, on, on, I plodded. By this time, more and more people were finding out what I was doing. A group of horrified Fundamentalist Christians told me that Satan wanted me to find out the truths of biblical history. "You are condemning yourself to Eternal Hell for trying to learn biblical history as truth!" They warned.

But I would not be detoured from the objective. It took me twenty years to reach success, resulting in my 444 page book, *Jesus and Moses Are Buried in India, Birthplace of Abraham and the Hebrews!* In my struggles to find out the truth "that would send me to Hell," I searched in libraries all over the United States. I spent more than ten thousand dollars, ordering books from India itself! Again, again, and again, I repeat: Nothing can stand up against *persistence!* Actually, there may be no such thing as "genius." *Persistence* makes it seem that there is!

Although you must rivet yourself to a problem until it is solved, you should not wrestle with it in the same rut keeping you from conquering it. Approach it from other angles. Review previous material to see if you have overlooked something. Consult other textbooks. If you can't solve the problem on your own, consult people knowledgeable in the subject, as a last resort.

> What you have been obliged to discover by yourself leaves a path in your mind, which you can use again when the need arises…The best way to learn anything is to discover it by yourself…for

efficient learning, the learner should discover by himself as large a fraction of the material to be learned as feasible under the given circumstances. (*Aphorisms;* by G. C. Lichtenberg.)

If you refuse to be persistent in struggling for what you want, you are doomed to fail from the start. Persistence and self-reliance are foundation stones of genius. Neglect them, and your hopes and dreams crumble to dust. Persistence and self-reliance separate the men from the boys; the girls from the women; the sheep from the shepherds; the peasants from the kings.

Ninety-five percent of all human beings behave as if failure were a golden treasure. When the going gets rough, they give up and gladly reach for the easy-to-attain goals of tragedy and failure, which demand only hypocritical tears of anguish from their humble slaves. In most cases, people can make failure seem fun by finding someone on whom or something on which to blame their lack of guts and persistence. It's interesting to follow the lives of losers, which are studies in the art of evading self-responsibility. While they are young, they blame their troubles on their teachers, poverty, race, nationality, government, society, or parents. Later on, they add the excuse of "I'm working so hard making a living and supporting a family that I have no time to grow as a person." Finally, they tack on the best excuse of all—old age. Always an excuse for failure and stupidity. Never one to remain persistent and self-reliant.

If you do decide to be persistent in working for your goals, don't be like a young lady I met a number of years ago. She told me: "No one is more determined than I to get a good education. My mind is totally riveted on that objective. Nothing on earth can stop me—if the government will pay my way!"

Ignorance and poverty are the favorite goals of mankind. Though nearly everyone—possibly, even *you*—is fiercely and jealously struggling desperately to become poor and ignorant, the field never seems to be overcrowded. Demand is great. Success in these fields is guaranteed! And you don't have to bother about study and effort.

What can you do to lose the cut-throat, worldwide competition to be ignorant and poor? Nothing is easier. Resolve—right now—never again to surrender—never again to find excuses for failure.

Actually, the formula for achieving genius and success is extremely simple. If you want to triple your intelligence, then triple your effort. This is something you can begin to do tomorrow at your job or in the classroom. Presto! Instant intelligence enhancement!

Chapter IV

The Causes of Most Mental Blockages

In my thirty years as a teacher, I found out that just as many potential geniuses have difficulty learning as do those having lower I.Q.'s. Ninety-five or more percent of humans exploit just two to five percent of their respective potentials. If the average or below person used more than five percent of his potential, he would stand head over heels over most humans. I have read research indicating that some races and ethnicities are less intelligent than others. If I fell in the category of a so-called "less intelligent" race, I don't think I'd worry overmuch. In fact, I wouldn't worry at all. Nearly all the members of the so-called "most intelligent" races are going around acting more like monkeys than the monkeys themselves do. What microscopic bit of gray matter I used would put me on top of them anyway!

Scientific studies prove that people with as little as one-tenth normal brain size are capable of genius-level performance. In a past issue of *Science,* John Lorber, a British pediatrician, discussed a hydrocephalic British university student with an I.Q. of 126, who obtained an honors degree in mathematics—with virtually no brain! Dr. Lorber said that we must rethink the assumption that the cortex performs all the "higher" tasks that make us human; some of the more primitive cerebral structures may carry out many of the functions now attributed only to the cortex. If a young man with hardly any brain can obtain an honors degree in mathematics, what do you think *YOU* can do?

In the little Kansas town where I grew up, we had, as most towns do, a town fool. He was so retarded that he didn't even know exactly who he was. Absolutely unteachable, he had never been to school or received any kind of academic training. It goes without saying that he could neither read, write, nor calculate. He couldn't feed, clothe, or bathe himself. He was a total vegetable in every way except one—he was an electronics genius! Every day, his sister drove him to a local radio repair shop where he expertly diagnosed the type of malfunction in the equipment entrusted to him—without instruments! After that, he chose the correctly coded replacements and made appropriate repairs. There are hundreds of thousands of idiot savants in the world—living proof that knowledge can be acquired without brains or schools. How else can we explain the fact that such people have access to certain specialized pools of knowledge? If a totally mindless idiot can repair complicated electronic equipment, how much more should you, a seeker with the intelligence to read and understand this book, be able to accomplish!

Chapter V

Meet Man's combination Friend-Enemy: The Genesis Mind!

Much of Modern Man's irrational and unhappiness-sickness-causing behavior stems from his non-awareness of his unthinking, instinctive, non-analytical self, which I call the Genesis Self. This self acts and reacts automatically to environmental stimuli only as Nature wants it to, regardless of what the thinking, reasoning self "believes" *(brainwashes itself to become a prize fool)* or concludes. Everyone and everything is here, not as an accident of careless lovemaking, but for a definite reason and purpose. Each of us fulfills this purpose at all hours of the day and night, although we may not be conscious that we are on stage and following a script. The part that most of us play in modern life may be, in theory and in fact, an illusion because the thinking, reasoning self appears to be blind and deaf to the part if plays within Nature. If we could only realize that we're not playing our parts correctly, perhaps we'd alter and improve our education and behavior. Brain research offers little hope of our ever achieving the Greek dictum of "Know thyself." Instead, results show that all we can do is choose ourselves. To do that, we must pick out certain appealing goals and objectives, and then let our brains get the job done.

If you were to get a good look at your true, unthinking self, you would probably be astonished and disappointed to discover that you are in no way an individual but just a vibrating, unrelenting mass of instinctive drives, which essentially makes you no different from horses, dogs, rats, snakes, coyotes, vultures, roses, worms, or any other kind of animal, fish, fowl, or plant. This instinctive, automaton-like mass constantly demands food and drink, genital gratification and reproduction of species, protection and sustenance of the family and tribe, protection of its food territories, communal food and drink sharing, recognition of its place in and importance to the territorial group, emotional awareness, and other ape-like *(believing)* factors. It interprets all environmental stimuli and conditions in the context of its primitive drives—no matter what you, I, or anyone else may "think" or "know." Not one molecule of this mass knows or cares about any of the 'creations" of the conscious "thinking" self: religion, education, ideals, morals, beliefs *(self-delusional strategies)*, attitudes, technologies, fads, styles, messiahs, gurus, politics, economics—or whatever. When you step outside, you tell yourself that you see and recognize homes, autos, beauty, art, planes, streets, TV sets, computers, etc. The Genesis Self, your *instinctive self,* sees only the jungle! Basically, the Genesis Self asks only a few questions about everything you possess, think, or observe: "Can I eat it? Can I hide behind it? Can I screw it? Can I trust it? Can I kill it? Can I run away from it?"

Some philosophers of old taught, and even some blindly religious people have told me, that Man would be better off acting and reacting instinctively, without using the powers of thought. I don't need to tell you that if we shed ourselves of our hard-won thinking and reasoning processes, this world would become the harshest of jungles in which only the strongest and most clever could survive. I am glad that Adam and Eve (mankind) got clever enough to escape from Eden, a place where Man did not yet know how to think of ways to make his environment and lot on earth less hazardous and abrasive. We are making some progress in that direction, but our ignorance of our instincts and the different levels of individual awareness still keep us in darkness. To reach our lofty ideal of "Paradise on Earth," we must be careful to develop the right kind of human culture and embrace only those thoughts and ideals which can help us create a more beautiful, benign world for all humans and other beings. On the other hand, we will reach that goal only if we give the

Genesis Self whatever it demands. Being Nature itself, it will never sur-render. All human problems, the gulf between the "haves" and "have-nots," social strife, crime, ill-health, learning problems, and any other thing that can be christened "problem," will continue to exist as long as Man refuses to satisfy all the demands of his unthinking, reasoning, instinctive mass—his Genesis Self! We must also come to understand that Nature does not demand that we actually live in the jungle in order to placate Her, as some primitive tribes and "Back-to-Naturists" preach. The Genesis Mass does not care what you do to meet its demands—or how. If a man wants a sexual partner, he can rape her—or he can court and marry her. If he is hungry, he can catch a chicken, tear it apart alive with his hands and gobble it down—or, he can raise it in a coop, kill it in a painless way, and fry it in a skillet. As for distributing food and wealth, a person can either get with a tribe, join them on the hunt, share the prey with the tribe, and, at the same time, give the biggest and best cuts of meat to those who did the most to bring down the prey—as many extremely primitive tribes do even today. Or, he can do this: he can give all his countrymen (the tribe) a fair share of food, drink, clothing, and shel-ter, simultaneously letting those who made this abundance possible (such as businessmen and industrialists) get the biggest shares,

What happens when the Genesis Mass senses that it is to be denied or thwarted in its attempts to satisfy its primitive drives? It feels fear, anger, and/or stress. If the fear, anger, or stress is prolonged, or applies to con-ditions and situations not really pertinent to the satisfaction of its instinctive needs: food, sex, territorial sovereignty, recognition, etc., the body becomes damaged and ceases to function effectively, happily, and healthfully. On a collective level, the organisms so deprived experience war, unemployment, social alienation, famine, political oppression, and a host of other ills.

Many ignorant and unobservant writers give animals more credit than they deserve. I have read books in which the authors stated that wild animals generally enjoy vibrant health, hardly ever get sick, and never kill or intimidate without reason. But just the opposite is true. Wild animals are much more disease-prone and vicious than humans, for they did not choose to leave Eden as we did. As a matter of fact, diseases, privations, senseless slaughter, and cruelty among animals of the same species keep most of them from dying of old age.

Some psychologists teach that stress is created by Man's intellectual systems. They preach that the domesticated or captive animals are the only ones showing the effects of social stress. The truth is that an animal caught in a stress-creating situation, either of Man's, Nature's, another animals' or its own making, often dies within hours after acquiring this "stress." One day, when my wife and I were walking in the desert, she came upon a wild pigeon. She caught it before it could escape. It died in less than ten minutes!

Equally foolish are the writers who glorify the so-called "noble savages." In today's politically correct United States, we've convinced many of our American Indians that they were better off living in the pristine state. Yet, many primitives who haven't yet been "taken over" by the niceties of this modern technological age, would give their jungles for the stresses that we of the technology-producing societies suffer. Because of the many tribes warring on one another constantly, desirous of enough security to at least sleep soundly at night, the fierce Northern Mexican tribes surrendered to a half-Spanish, half-Aztec *conquistador* and only 100 Spanish soldiers. They preferred slavery in the White man's silver mines to the stresses of their primitive environment. I have heard songs and stories about the so-called non-stressful attitudes of the Mexican people, among whom I have lived most of my life. Yet, they live in one of the most stress-ridden societies I have ever known. Mexican immigrants to this country have told me that back in their homelands they always felt uneasy and insecure. Yet, after crossing over to the United States, they feel a strange sense of security and inner peace.

Chapter VI

Turn Racism into Favoritism—
Toward You!

Father Gracián prescribed the perfect remedies for anyone wanting to change racisim from a curse into a priceless benefit:

> *Avoid the defects of your country.* Water shares the good and bad qualities of the beds through which it runs; people share those of the region where they are born. Some owe more than others to their mother country or city, for they were born under favorable skies. No country, not even the most refined, has ever escaped some innate defect or other, and these weaknesses are seized on by neighboring countries as defense or consolation. It is a triumph to correct, or at least dissimulate, such national faults. By doing so, you will be revered as unique among your people, for what is least expected is most valued. Other defects are caused by one's lineage, condition, occupation, and by the times. If all these defects come together in one person, and no care is taken to foresee and correct them, they produce an intolerable monster.

> *Keep changing your style of doing things.* Vary your methods. This will confuse people, especially your rivals, and awaken their curiosity and attention. If you will always act on your first intention, others will foresee it and thwart it. It is easy to kill the bird that flies in a straight line, but not one that changes its line of flight. Don't always act on your second

intention either; do something twice, and others will discover the ruse. Malice is ready to pounce on you; you need a good deal of sublety to outwit it. The consummate player never moves the piece his opponent expects him to, and, less still, the piece he wants him to move.

Father Gracián said, *Avoid the defects of your country.* If the members of a certain race, nationality, or creed are suffering from some forms of discrimination, it is a fact that a great many members of that group are engaging in certain types of behaviors of which the dominant group in a country disapprove. A person wanting to free himself of stereotypes must find out first just what those stereotypes are. After that, he must project behaviors opposite to those that the dominant social group expects him to exhibit.

Father Gracián also recommended: *Keep changing your style of doing things.* For example, if many members of your group like to dress in flamboyant, threatening clothing, become a more conservative dresser. If they like loud, ear-splitting music, choose softer, more pleasant music. If their speech is generally substandard, polish up your own. If you are expected to be a slave to boxing, basketball, or football, become a chess champion. When the dominant group notices that your behavior is not what they expect it to be, they will come to value you highly as an exceptional person and a credit to your race. You will even get positions and recognition that you may not really deserve. Naturally, your astuteness will excite jealousy and envy from those of your own group, who may not want you to forge ahead, but don't forget: Father Gracián also said, *Do not play to lose. Do not die of another's misery.*

When I first went to live and study in Mexico, I noticed right away that an undercurrent of racism against *gringos* existed there. Although there was naturally much resentment for my being from a more prosperous country, Americans were also disliked for not liking to discuss controversial and intellectually stimulating subjects, especially those of the "politically incorrect" variety, for liking loud music, for acting unseemly in public places, for being generally Protestant, for being clannish and speaking only English, and for a number of other factors. I quit being Protestant and joined the Catholic Church. I also changed my mode of dress. I started wearing a suit and tie everywhere. In the cities, I wore Spanish berets; straw hats in the countryside. I even taught myself to enjoy discussing all kinds of subjects, even those Americans generally regard as "politically incorrect." I also became fluent in Spanish, plus making several other changes in my attitudes and behaviors. Many of my own countrymen started regarding me as a traitor, but I didn't want to lock myself within the American colony; I wanted to enjoy Mexico within the bosom of its own people and culture. The rewards were not long in coming. The Mexicans appreciated the fact that I changed some of my behaviors, even my religion, in order to please them. I never lacked for invitations to parties and important social functions.

I had another friend who also sought thorough assimilation with the Mexicans. He did not eventually return to the United States as I did. A few years ago, when my wife and I were walking in a corridor of the *Metro* (Mexico City's subway system), we entered a bookstore. I was surprised to find my old friend Bill there. He told me that he was the owner of a small chain of bookstores in Mexico City. He had also married a Mexican woman with whom he raised several children. He said that he had not returned to the United States in thirty years. Noticing that his English had deteriorated dramatically, I said, "Bill, don't tell me you've given up your citizenship as well!"

Bill started whimpering. In his now deficient English, he sobbed, "No, Gene, I never give up that." Would an American traitor make such a statement?

In those days, the American colony shunned those Americans who fraternized too intimately with Mexicans. But we didn't fret too much. Quote me on this: *Latinos have more fun!*

One of the wisest and most unforgettable characters I ever knew in my life was a Black Alabaman named Ulester Mims. Early in life, Ulester decided that Blacks could overcome both overt and covert racism only by privately and publicly exhibiting all the virtues and qualities that Whites admired in human beings. He was also careful to demonstrate behaviors contradicting all the stereotypes that Whites had of Blacks. All the Whites loved him and sought his company. Les told me that back in Alabama, he was the only Black in town welcome as a visitor in White homes. He was no less popular in Mexico. Les found out that Mexicans believe that if a Black person will enter their homes and sweep it with a new broom, they'll always have good luck. Les always kept small toy brooms on hand. Whenever he made a new Mexican friend, Les would enter his home with one of those little brooms and sweep it symbolically.

Les often went too far to please Whites. He pretended to hate fried chicken and watermelon. I said to him one day, "Les, you're making too many sacrifices. Many of us Whites are also convinced that fried chicken and ice-cold watermelon are God's gift to mankind."

Needless to say, Les wasn't overly popular with his own kind. One day, a Black acquaintance scolded him for being too cooperative with Whites. Les defended himself, saying, "Hell, Joe, I believe that if you can't beat them, then join them!"

Some people don't like to free themselves from racism, using Les's one hundred percent effective formula. They say, "Why must we try harder than anyone else? Why must we be better than anyone else in order to attain equality? Why us?"

Why not YOU? Being everybody's punching bag never produces benefits for anyone, not even for the privileged castes. Look at things this way: I don't have to tell you that most of the members of the dominant race are just pretending to be better than everyone else. If, by just pretending to be superior to everyone else, they have been able to enjoy the good life, wouldn't someone who is REALLY better than anyone else get even bigger slices of the pie of life? So what's wrong with being better than everyone else?

Chapter VII

Why Mother Nature Seems to Want You to Remain Stupid!

I'm fond of saying that anyone wanting to learn the truth of life should drive on the California freeways. The Genesis Self of a particularly stupid person, of which there is an infinity in the world, thinks *(fools itself)* that if it can pass everyone on the freeway, or reach a particular stoplight ahead of all the other cars, it's going to be the first to catch a rabbit or a deer for supper. It says to itself, "Not only will I be the first to catch the deer, the grateful tribe will hail me as a hero and give me the biggest and best pieces of meat tonight. My family and I will eat our fill!"

If it falls behind on the freeway or fails to reach a red light before the other cars, it thinks it's going to bed hungry that night. This fear of being last fills it with anger and stress. It is this primitive fear of not catching a deer on time that is the reason for most reckless driving and road-rage on our nation's freeways.

Back in high school, my teacher of salesmanship taught this secret of why some people who enter a store pretend to be in a hurry. They want to feel important. They want to think they're going to be the first hunter to bring down a deer. He said that when such people enter a store, a smart salesman will treat them as V.I.P.'s, helping them get what they're after as quickly as possible. Such people will be so grateful that they'll become regular customers in the store.

This world has been here for millions of years; Man for even less. Scientists are saying that Europoids (Whites) have been here for only twenty two thousand years. Modern Man has not been around long enough to know the difference between what is jungle and what is not. Therefore, for the next few thousand years, possibly more, we must be aware that our instinctive, primitive needs and drives are in the "driver's seat." As of this date, Nature knows nothing of book-learning and planning for the future. All she sees in books and schoolrooms is a barren territory housing strange symbols and nutrition-poor objects like chairs, chalkboards, pencils, and notebooks. She becomes alarmed that a student will starve to death if he just sits (hunts) in this barren territory. She fills him with impatience, even paralyzing his mind with a fear of starving to death, in such a sterile environment. Fear, anger, apprehension, and stress decrease blood circulation to the brain, thus preventing the mind from working efficiently. The person who blocks up mentally when trying to learn is just receiving danger signals from Nature. She wants him to close his text, get out of that classroom, and seek a hunting ground with real flesh-and-blood prey. For this reason, poor, needy children, whose families must struggle hard for their daily bread, tend to do worse academically than those from more affluent backgrounds. The unconscious self of a rich child knows that its nutritional needs will always be satisfied—even in a barren classroom (hunting ground). During my thirty years as a classroom teacher, I made numerous investigations proving that slow learners and potential dropouts are in reality people who can't unfreeze their minds and relax. The problem is especially serious among immigrant children who lived at subsistence level in their countries of origin. On the other hand, immigrant children who enjoyed some degree of affluence in their respective homelands were generally a delight to have in classroom situations.

I would now like for you to ponder the riddle that makes people fearful of being adventurous or of trying new ways of thinking and doing.

When a person decides to seek riches, power, and greater freedom, why do the people closest to him, even his family, generally fail to support him? Why will they poke fun at him, call him stupid, and do everything possible to keep him from reaching his lofty goals?

This is what their inner selves are saying to them: "He wants to catch the deer first and get a bigger piece of meat for supper. He may not share the deer with us. We may starve to death!"

Two restaurants are on the same block. One is nothing more than a "greasy spoon" where the employees get minimum wages with no tips, are treated as slaves and constantly live in fear that their cruel boss will fire them. The other restaurant caters to an economically privileged, free-spending clientele; the chefs are well-paid professionals; the waiters make several hundred dollars a day in tips. Yet, the cooks and waiters in the "greasy spoon" are as qualified and efficient as those in the luxury restaurant. What force keeps them enslaved? What keeps them from just walking down the street and getting better jobs?

Their Genesis Selves are warning them: "You must be satisfied with what little food lies in this food-gathering territory. If you leave here for a strange territory, its occupants may not let you enter it."

The mailorder business has to be the world's riskiest way to make money. Advertising costs eat up most of the profits; profits are marginal. Yet, people will do everything short of murder to get a foothold in this business. The government warns the public to beware of the rip-off homework schemes sold by many unscrupulous mailorder concerns, such as stuffing envelopes, and the like. Even so, the homework con-artists keep on prospering. I get no less than a dozen such offers a day on the Internet. Why do people yearn to make money at home?

Their Genesis Selves say to them: "If you can get the prey to come to this cave, you'll avoid the insecurity of the jungle."

Another scheme that enriches many con-artists is the "get-rich-report" telling people how they can become millionaires by using other people's money. Why do people fear to risk their own money on new businesses?

Again, a person's primitive instinctual being whispers to him, "Let other people do the hunting for you!"

In Mexico, I knew a group of Indians who lived on a high, cold, arid, wind-swept mountain. From their lofty crags, they could look down on lush, tropical valleys teeming with animals and vegetable foods. Although they were starving to death, they were afraid to walk the four or five hours necessary to reach a jungle paradise. Why did they choose to starve to death in their icy hell? They did it for the same reasons that the personnel of the "greasy spoon" restaurant were afraid to look for better jobs.

Medical scientists have actually proven that drastic, new changes in an adult's lifestyle, even beneficial changes, can make him sick. Why? Over and over, I repeat: Man is a territorial animal. He is afraid to leave his territory because if he does, and things don't go well for him when he's out of his element, the "tribe" may not let him come back home.

I know a young Mexican woman who travels one hour each way every day to work in a motel in a nearby town for only six hours a day, with minimum wages and no benefits. Yet, here in this little town where she and I live, she could get a job any day of the week, receiving eight and more hours of labor every day, better pay, and medical benefits. When I asked her why she refused to get a job in this town, she answered: "Let's suppose that something happens to make me lose a job here in town. Naturally, the owner of the motel will be angry with me and won't let me go back to work for him. Therefore, I've decided that a bird in the hand is worth two in the bush."

It's a fact that the universe contains limitless abundance and energy. We have infinitely abundant reserves of solar, wind, and cosmic energies; methods for making methane gas cheaply from vegetable wastes, sewage, etc., and the technology to use them right now. Yet, the alternate energy sciences are not getting much public and governmental support. Why? Again, I repeat over and over: Nature encourages us to be territorial.

A recent film showed how a group of English and Irish prisoners were jailed in the hold of a dirty sailing ship bound for Australia which was originally a 19th Century penal colony. The ship's captain tortured them daily, giving them inadequate rations of food and water; several women died of disease. Yet, when they reached Australia, they were afraid to go ashore. Can't you guess why?

Along with the innate human fear of not being able to hunt, or the dread of hunting in unknown or barren territories like schoolrooms, Nature keeps people instinctively chained to their home territories where they are more experienced and skilled in exploiting local food sources. When a person dares to be different from his peers, Nature fills him with fear of the unknown. "Don't go," She whispers. "That unknown territory may house warlike people who will kill you, ferocious beasts, unfamiliar foods, barren desserts, and the like. Be like everybody else here. Don't do anything to endanger the precious security you already have, however meager it may be."

When the principal of a school where I once taught learned that I had started a business, he told me to give it up. "My teachers make an average of $11,000 a year. That's enough." The poor fellow didn't have sense enough to know that Nature was using him to keep me in line. Had he known, he really would have said, "How do you know that the new territory in which you are entering has any deer? Better to stay here where you can at least eat rabbits. Also, if you do find a lot of deer in the new territory, the tribe may follow you, and I won't be chief any more. I'll have to be satisfied with the smallest pieces of meat like the other lesser warriors."

People wonder why I have always disliked most competitive games and team sports. I scorn most team sports and games because they are Nature's way of encouraging us to preserve our basic predatory instincts. A runner who wins a race thinks he has won a race. Nature thinks that he has caught a rabbit for his "tribe." Since Nature decrees that the most skillful hunter should get the biggest and best pieces of rabbit, many people work hard to become champion athletes.

Why do girls seem to fall for "the guys on the team?" Food is essential for life. Our athletes (hunters and warriors), according to our instincts, risk life and limb keeping invaders out of our food territory (the goal post), and competing for food with other tribes in our area. When our team (hunters and warriors) win, we get plenty to eat. When they lose, we go hungry. That's why after some sports events, many of the spectators who supported the losers go wild and commit mayhem. You would, too, if you knew you were going to bed hungry after the game!

The girls want team members (hunters and warriors) for lovers and mates because such unions convince their Genesis Selves that they'll always be well protected and fed.

As my old high school P.E teacher always told me, *"We must always support the team!"* Another of Nature's "yes-men," he really meant, "Let's support those who hunt for our food and fight the enemies who threaten our villages and food-gathering territory." Naturally, we must pay high salaries to our athletes. Anything to encourage them to keep on bringing home our food and protecting the village. It goes without saying that we must make fun of "nerds," "dorks," and "geeks" who prefer to use their minds instead of dancing around campfires (pep rallies), shaking spears, and using brute force. People who live in the jungle, and that includes nearly all of us, think that only brute gorilla force produces the best results. After all, isn't that what we were taught back in high school? *You must always support the team!*

As if territorial instincts weren't enough to keep people from being unique, Nature uses other ploys to pressure 95% of all humans to accept the burden of inferiority and be "just like everybody else." Man is a social animal, naturally programmed to interact with groups and follow a minority of leaders. If most humans were born free of strong follower instincts, the human condition might become much more anarchic, chaotic, and savage than it is now. In fact, mankind would probably become extinct. To make sure that human society has more Indians than chiefs, only a few people are born free of the herd instinct. They feel little or none of Nature's gravitational pull downward. The rest of us aren't so lucky. When Nature notices that one of the "Indians" is employing the tools for success: job dedication; persistence; goals; individuality; ambition; development of virtue and high moral standards;

culture; vocabulary; grammar; mathematics, etc.; she fills him with unconscious fear, self-doubts, aversion to boredom and time-consuming activities. She will even cause friends and family members to dog-pile him and insist that he be a sheep for the rest of his life. "Why can't you be just like everybody else?" As I have said previously, the principal wanting me to abandon my business venture really wanted to say, "You have me for a chief. I haven't yet died or become too old and sickly for you to challenge my authority. You must keep on being an 'Indian!'"

Another way Nature keeps us in line is to make us feel "ethnocentric" or the attitude that we must remain firmly fixed in a particular language and ethnic group. The devilish disease of "national culture," and the insanity forcing people to value it more highly than morality, values, individual initiative, and mental-social-physical-economic well-being are the last weapons of racist-social-economic-political knavery. If you want to become free of all the chains keeping you from rising to your highest potential, you will have to free yourself of all animal territorial and tribal instincts. This is more easily said than done, I know.

Here's an example of how "cultural peculiarities" hold people back: Although modern Mexican culture is changing rapidly, the old idea that studious men cannot possibly be manly is still very much alive in that country. During one summer, when my family and I were spending our yearly three months vacation in Acapulco, the owner of the small hotel where we stayed noticed that I often spent part of my afternoons studying mathematics. Thinking that my love of study had rendered me impotent, he started prancing in front of my wife and bragging, "No one can ever accuse *me* of reading a book!"

During another of our summer vacations, my car broke down outside the port of Mazatlán. We had a tow truck take it to the Plymouth agency there. However, since my Plymouth was really a Japanese Mitsubishi in disguise, the agency didn't have the part I needed to get the car repaired. I sent my wife to the United States on a bus, to pick up the part. During her absence, I ate every day in a little restaurant at the local market place. The young seventeen years old waitress who served me my meals demonstrated a high level of intelligence. I said to her one day, "You should go back to school and get an education so that you can become more than a mere waitress."

She answered, "I'd love to, but I'm too poor to pay for my tuition and books."

"I don't agree. When I was downtown today, I noticed that the local government-operated trade school is recruiting students in the plaza, promising that tuition and books will be free. A wide variety of interesting, well-paid careers are being taught."

She said, "I'll tell my parents about this when I go home today."

The next day, when she served my lunch, I asked, "What did your parents say about what we were talking about yesterday?"

"My mother thinks it is good for me to continue my education. But Dad said I can't continue with my schooling. He says that women don't need an education because they're just going to get married and raise kids."

I answered, "Young lady, in all respect to your father, tell him that I said he's a stupid asshole. Women also have dreams of self-fulfillment! This world is for everyone; not just for men."

During my career as a high school teacher, I noticed that my highly motivated Black students were often bullied, mocked and mistreated by peers of their own race. They were accused of acting "White." One day, I talked with a group of these bullies. "You're the ones who are acting 'White.' Many Whites don't want Blacks to progress in life. By intimidating Black students who do want to make something of themselves, you are doing exactly what those Whites who are bigoted want you to do! Why don't you quit acting 'White'?"

On another occasion, I overheard one of my Mexican wife's nephews insult his brother who was an excellent student in school: "All you are is just a White boy."

I quickly ran up to his brother and embraced him affectionately: "Oh, Roberto, I didn't know that we Whites act and think the way you do. Now that I know, I feel really good about myself and my fellow 'Whites.'" Of course, I said that with tongue in cheek. In my thirty years' experience as a teacher, I noticed that "acting White'" is the last thing most "White" kids do. Only the East Asian kids act "White."

Is your particular national, racial, cultural, economic and/or social group lapping up the cream of life? Or must it be content with the scraps falling from the master's table? If you aren't lapping up cream, perhaps you should examine your "unique cultural heritage" and "tribal affiliations." Maybe they aren't good enough. Maybe they're holding you back. Maybe you'd better off being your own combination chief and tribe of one. Think of what I said in the last chapter about escaping from negative racial and cultural stereotypes.

Psychologists and researchers have long known that modern Man's primitive Genesis Self reacts unrealistically to the false threats encountered in modern living. They are even preaching that anger and many aspects of fear are unacceptable reactions in a civilized, highly technological environment. Unfortunately, such reactions will always be unacceptable to Nature at this level of human evolution. She cares not for the opinions of psychologists. At our present evolutionary level, Nature can't be forced to mend her ways. For the next millennium or more, she will continue to react as if we humans had no education or thoughts. A certain amount of stress must always accompany modern Man's ever-widening separation from Eden. Only a consummate fool would truly want to return to an Eden where humans must uncomplainingly let lions and other predators rip generous gobs of fresh meat from their already pain-wracked rear ends. There is no way out of our predicament—only a way up in it. Dr. Barbara Brown, a famous psychiatrist and writer, penned the following observation: "I contend…that the instinctual, physiological arousal of physical mechanisms, developed over eons as animal species have evolved, is no longer necessary to defend against physical assaults to social well-being." Yet, as I've just told you, Man, whom Nature created to belong to and cooperate with groups, is eternally bound by that same Nature to react physically and emotionally against assaults to social well-being. For the next few hundred or thousand years—perhaps for the next hundred thousand years—she will continue to reject textbooks, paper, and pencils within her realm. All we can do is control the degree of impact and influence that Nature has on us. We approach (but never reach) the threshold of total liberation only in direct relation to our individual skills in the art and science of deep relaxation. If we can learn how to control the degree to which we must be tied to our respective instinctual natures, we will be able to virtually eliminate many learning problems, illnesses, extreme poverty, undesirable social problems, and most of anything else classifiable as "terrible."

Instead of continuing to suffer frustrations and mental blocks in learning situations, you must learn instead to relax automatically and unconsciously whenever you meet a crisis which doesn't actually threaten your ability to defend your life, get food, and appease your other instinctive drives. The more deeply a person learns to relax his body and mind at will, the greater his ability to learn. My statements stand on solid scientific foundations. Investigations by Georgetown University consultant Bernard Brown and psychiatry professor Lillian Rosenbaum reported that children's I.Q. test performance drops significantly as stress levels increase. A proper understanding of how stress lowers I.Q. could lead to new approaches to the measurement of intelligence. According to them, stress management and biofeedback techniques could directly affect intelligence levels. In a *Science Digest* interview (10-82), Rosenbaum said, "…Mozart and Einstein might have produced five to ten percent better if their stress levels had been effectively reduced." Right now, Man's mind has not advanced to the point where he can see that I.Q. and college entry tests aren't valid—or even necessary. Concerned that their tests may reveal that they aren't "good enough" to hunt down deer and defend the tribe adequately, thus notifying the tribe that they don't qualify for sufficient food and protection within the tribe, nearly everyone tests far below his potential. All I.Q, college entry, and other similar tests should be outlawed because they cause both the individual taking the test and society as a whole to condemn humanity to an unflinching caste system fully as frightful as the one in India.

Chapter VIII

How to Keep the Genesis Self in Permanent Hibernation

When I was in the eighth grade, one of my friends said to me, "The teacher says you have a high I.Q. You scored 120 on the test." The truth is that my I.Q. was probably even higher. However, by the time I reached the eighth grade, I had not only developed a fear of classrooms, but I had a low opinion of my own intellectual capabilities—and still do. That's why I'm always trying to improve them. Regardless of what the positive-thinking gurus say, you'll learn in this book why *no one should ever believe in himself!*

My troubles started back in kindergarten. Until I reached the first grade, my memory was photographic. In plays and skits at church, I memorized everyone else's part along with mine. When a fellow actor made mistakes, I would put my hand over his mouth, repeating his part correctly to the audience. Mother wrote in my baby book that I preferred books to toys and games, treating the former with great reverence. I also exhibited exceptional musical talent, but an incident in first grade nearly froze my abilities for life.

Just before finishing kindergarten, I took a little test to help the teacher decide whether I should be placed with a class of intelligent students (the A class) or with a group of alleged dullards (the B class) the following September. I had to draw a rabbit. Being an awkward lefty, I naturally failed the rabbit test and was assigned to B class. The B teacher soon discovered that I was different from the other students. I learned to read well in less than six weeks, mastered the readers available at my level, and bought more complicated books from home. I also helped the teacher control the children and even led them in singing. The teacher persuaded the administration to transfer me to A class. I know now that I should have remained in B class. The transition to A was too rapid and traumatic. Though beyond most of the A group in reading, I was far behind them in writing and elementary mathematics. Failing to realize that I was not yet ready to perform mathematically, the A teacher sent me to the board to solve some beginning addition problems. Something happened at that moment to numb my mind, condemning me to be a poor student throughout grade school and part of high school. I was also treated as a criminal for being left-handed (the real reason why I had been sent to B class first). Even the superintendent came to yell at me for being left-handed. I'll never forget how he pulled the pencil out of my left hand and placed it on my right palm. Closing my fingers tightly around the pencil, he screamed, "This is the hand you should write with!"

To make matters worse, my peers made fun of me for being such a good piano player. To please them, I gave up music altogether for a number of years.

I also had a natural dislike of being part of a group and group sports. At the beginning of seventh grade, our homeroom teacher tried to recruit us for group sports. I stood up and frankly told the class, "I refuse to chase leather balls over a field or drop them into a basket." The children then began to call me a coward, but that didn't last long. I was more than willing to sign up for boxing and wrestling.

Yet, I demonstrated academic excellence out of the classroom. I almost lived in our public library. I read nearly everything it had to offer. By the time I was out of high school, I could locate any non-fiction book there without having to search in the index file.

Although I have accomplished much academically over the years, the wounds I received from that agonizing and traumatic transferral to A class, the intolerance of my left-handedness, peer pressures to give up my piano lessons, and the criticism I had to endure for not wanting to be a herd animal, continue to cause my mind and soul to bleed. Those experiences cursed me with emotional problems. For example, whenever I find myself in an insecure situation, I frequently stutter. Whenever I must learn or choose to learn something new, my mind literally freezes until I rid myself of my negative beliefs *(stupid, unproven attitudes)* about myself. I also tend to feel insecure when surrounded by highly talented and accomplished individuals. Not only do I not want them to notice how utterly ignorant I am, they also remind me of the group I had to confront on my first day in A class.

Fortunately, in my typing and Spanish classes, I discovered that by making frequent repetitions and practicing persistence, I could rise above my learning and emotional problems. From then on, I became a good student and lost my fear of classrooms. From then on, people told me, "Gene, you're just naturally a good student!"

A person wanting to improve himself intellectually must additionally trash all preconceptions and attitudes he has about the skills and concepts he wants to master. He needs to stop "believing" *(self deception)* that mathematics is hard; that physics is only for "nerds," etc. Simply stated, a subject is "what it is;" not what you think or believe *(guess)* it is. If we humans trained ourselves to see something for what it is, not brainwashing ourselves to "believe" it is hard, for nerds only, etc., etc., etc., geniuses would become the rule; not the exception. A good part of this book will concentrate heavily on helping readers develop this "existential" type of mentality. Take that information seriously, for it holds simultaneously the key to individual and collective greatness! And here's something else that will knock the foundations from much of what you've been brainwashed to accept: *You'll find out why you even have to quit believing in yourself!*

My lifetime of researching my own learning problems and those of hundreds of other kindred souls has proven to me that almost every human being, especially he who silently and meekly grovels before and labors for cruel bosses and leaders, is carrying the same chains that began to bind my mind in A class. Even animals suffer from this same bondage occasionally. It's the devilish scourge called stress. No one can ever be truly intelligent, healthy, or happy until he weakens the instinctual drives pressuring him to be an humble member of the herd. Deep relaxation exercises will weaken the force of Nature's pleas that you live out your life as a stupid cow or sheep.

The type of relaxation you need to master is far more profound than the simple act of lying down on a bed and repeating over and over: "My toes are completely limp; now my legs; now my facial muscles, etc." This type of "relaxing" is recommended by those ignorant but well-meaning self-improvement teachers who, though they have stumbled upon one of the secrets of salvation, do not yet know that a person can make himself actually think and feel he is relaxed but yet be drowning in a sea of stress. Man, even in ideal situations, always thinks, believes *(fools himself)*, acts, and feels as if he were in a dream world. Things are always far from being exactly what he thinks, feels, or wants them to be. You see, Truth, as the thinking mind wants to perceive it, is never an absolute but an approximation at best. The mathematical art called calculus proves that we can approach but never reach any limit. Man will never know absolute truth. Absolute truth is the exclusive property of Nature, and I strongly suspect that not even the ever-expanding universe or Nature knows what absolute truth is.

Thanks to the ever-expanding developments in electronics technology, each of us can quit depending on the illusions thrown up by our minds and deceitful conscious and unconscious beliefs *(devils)* and feelings. Delicate electronic instruments, the tools of a new, rapidly growing science of human awareness technology, called *Biofeedback,* can note the subtle chemical and physiological changes accompanying profound relaxation states, which the thinking mind can never feel or perceive.

When I was in my fourth year of teaching, I accidentally discovered how Man's ignorance of the Genesis Mass stifles the learning processes.

Since I didn't have enough Spanish students to fill in a school day, the administration gave me a remedial English class composed of chronic failures and uninterested, potential dropouts. Whenever I described to them a point of grammar and asked them to write sentences emphasizing that point, they became unusually nervous. The tension leaping from their tortured minds and nervous systems almost made the atmosphere crackle. They desperately conferred with one another in a frantic attempt to translate my descriptions and examples into concepts they could understand. As they bled, groaned, groped, grasped, gasped, and stumbled for answers or fought to evade them, they became almost unmanageable. Their reactions ranged all the way from actual confessions of fear and uncertainty to demonstrations of bravado and aggression—typical attitudes of people confronting danger-provoking, threatening situations. Some of the students even rejoiced in my inability to reach down and yank them out of the herd: "You can't teach me nothin'!"

Most educators think that unmanageable students hate to sit down all day. They are wrong. A problem student will usually stay seated and calm throughout the school day, provided he doesn't have to deal with threats to his Genesis Mass.

While watching my students' Genesis Mass react hysterically to what it regarded as threats, I remembered the terror I first felt as a beginning teacher, when I had to memorize 150 or more new names each semester. I later discovered that I could memorize those names and faces in less than a week by relaxing and no longer worrying about having to learn them, just like the old man who had no problem sleeping with his beard until he started wondering how he did it. And then I saw the light! My mind leaped back to the most terrifying moment in my life—that horrible first day in A class. Eureka! I said to myself. I have it. The answer is and ever shall be *deep relaxation!*

I then started doing research on the part that fear, anger, and stress play in suffocating and paralyzing human intelligence. Fortunately, I didn't have to dig too deep. Many researchers and scientists, far more qualified than I, had already laid the groundwork.

What surprised me in my research was the relatively little importance that previous investigators had given to their discoveries of how stress chokes off most students' ability to learn. Only now, through the science of biofeedback, are researchers beginning to understand that those who have mastered the art of deep relaxation have the keys to the universe in their hands.

Chapter IX

Crushing the Tyranny of Beliefs—Man's Next Step Upward in Human Evolution!

Up to this point, you have probably noticed that I keep hinting that "belief" is mankind's most primitive, rock-bottom thinking mechanism. Don't become bored with this constant repetition. From now on, I stop hinting, and tell it like it is—also repetitively. You have inherited millenniums of a type of baggage that must be trashed—now! Take your medicine.

Measure Your Own Degree of Mental Evolution.

Are you a full-fledged member of civilized Society? Or do you still have both feet in the jungle and/or the animal world? How ignorant are you? How educated or uneducated are you? How stupid or intelligent? The following test will give you an astonishingly accurate and scientific measurement of your inner evolution and accomplishments. The test is simple: Compare the ideas, behaviors, and things in which you believe *(guess)* exist with those you know exist. For example, you may know that computers and electrical energy exist, but you may "believe *(proudly maintain the obsession that you're a fool)*" that your next door neighbors are bad, or that rabbits' feet bring good luck. The greater amount of beliefs a person acquires and defends, the closer he is to the jungle.

At this point in human evolution, no matter how many abbreviations of advanced college degrees you may have listed after your name, the sum total of your knowledge is almost non-existent, compared with the things you believe and don't believe. Non-belief is just a negative form of believing: *I believe "not."* Furthermore, I go so far as to declare: *All—one hundred percent—of the denotations, connotations, variations of, and expressions of "belief,"* **as Modern Man now understands the term**, *never did, don't, and never will serve any useful, constructive purpose in human affairs. If we humans continue to employ "belief,"* **as we presently understand it**, *as a twin brother and ally of truth, we are, both individually and collectively, doomed to eventual destruction and extinction. There is nothing on earth quite so evil as the act of "believing,"* **according to modern concepts of the term**.

The human organism is conditioned naturally to recognize reality only. When you force your organism to accept non-truths as realities, tremendously destructive forces are released in the body and psyche, eventually destroying the "True Believer". This is true even with positive beliefs, as well as with religious and political beliefs. Can you afford to keep on worshiping the God of Belief?

Review the reasons I gave in the previous chapters for human stupidity, ignorance, bestiality, failure, inability to learn, wars, misunderstandings, need, poverty, suffering of all kinds, and other factors preventing human beings from reaching their maximum respective potentials. Notice that they *ALL* stem from different forms of negative beliefs, attitudes and convictions, many of which sprout from Man's instinctive, animal Genesis Self! Because *belief is mankind's lowest and most primitive form of judging and thinking, almost sub-mental, all of us* are compelled to express beliefs *most of the time.* However, if we classify beliefs *(stupid illusions)* as equal with knowledge, truth, natural law, and science, giving them more importance than they warrant, they become the parents of most known and unknown forms of evil.

There is an old saying, "While I don't accept your beliefs about certain things, I would die for your right to believe them." The hellish "serial killer" who perpetuated the lethal, passive acceptance and tolerance of beliefs, **as we now understand the term**, gave a green light to the powers of darkness. Yes, I know the admonitions in all religions: *"Believe," and you shall be saved."* But when men like Christ exhorted mankind to "believe in me," **was he conveying to his followers the denotations and connotations that "belief" now conveys to us?** Other biblical statements attributed to Christ indicate that he was not. Word meanings change over the millenniums; "belief" didn't change for the best.

Dictionaries provide the following definition of "belief:"

> *"...an opinion or conviction...confidence in the truth of existence of something not immediately susceptible to rigorous proof...conclusion, persuasion, assurance...Acceptance of or confidence in, an alleged fact or body of facts as true or right without positive knowledge or proof; certainty or unquestioning belief and positiveness in one's own mind that something is true; conviction or settled, profound, or earnest belief that something is right; doctrine; dogma, etc."*

Never again forget the above definition—not even for a moment!

Humans also express "belief *(public admission of their own stupidity)*" by describing particular objects, beings, behaviors and concepts as existential realities. Examples: *Joe is a lousy person. Russians are untrustworthy. The Mojave desert is ugly. God loves you. God condemns you to hell for your unrighteousness in His eyes.* These are the most dangerous of all the other ways of expressing beliefs, for they imply absolute knowledge and certainty.

Many times, existential "beliefs *(insisting that faulty, unreal ideas are genuine)*" can be proven invalid by reconstructing them in simple syllogisms. Just recently, I told a well-educated friend that my wife and I had recently walked out of a cinema featuring a certain movie showing homosexuals making love and caressing one another publicly. He growled at me viciously: "This means that you are homophobic."

Chafing from such an unfair accusation, I answered, "But some of my best friends are homosexuals."

He said, "That's a typical defense one gets from racists and bigots: 'Some of my best friends are African-Americans; some of my best friends are Jewish; some of my best friends are Mexicans; blah, blah, blah.'"

Had he used syllogisms to analyze his "sure indications" of racists and bigots, he wouldn't have made such an illogical accusation: *If some of my best friends are homosexuals, then I hate homosexuals.* The reverse of the preceding statement would be, *If I hate homosexuals, then some of my best friends are homosexuals.*

The above syllogisms lead us to some curious corollaries (correlations or propositions that are incidentally proved in providing other propositions): *If I have no homosexual friends, then I love homosexuals;* or, *If I have some friends of all races, creeds, and sexual orientations, then I hate all human beings;* or, *If I have no friends of any race, creed, or sexual orientation, then I love all human beings;* or, *If I'm Grand Dragon of the Ku Klux Klan, I am entirely free of racial bigotry!*

I discussed the accusation that I was homophobic with a homosexual friend who had been my "best man" when my wife and I got married. He told me that as a male homosexual, he could not bear to watch love-making between lesbians and could barely tolerate public acts of heterosexual affection. My homosexual friend's comments convinced me that many people may become generally disgusted by observing expressions of love between persons having sexual proclivities opposite to theirs. However, such repulsion need not indicate hate and rejection of such people.

I'll never forget what a Black friend of mine told me before he died of cancer: "Gene, I want you to know that I have always admired you for your lack of racial prejudice."

Bill, I answered, "Perhaps I've turned into a racist over the years. I must admit that I feel fearful whenever I come upon a group of young black men wearing baggy trousers lopping down over their butts and listen to their loud, vulgar, sub-standard speech and rapping."

Bill answered. "Gene, that's not racism. That's just a commonsense will to survive. I, too, am afraid of them."

Could it be that a person can observe people different than he and see the good as well as the bad?

If you could right now be transported to the most backward areas of this earth, you'd discover that the whole lives of the inhabitants therein are geared to beliefs and non-beliefs, leaving very little, if any, room for actual demonstrable knowledge. The more backward and uncivilized a tribe, the more beliefs *(unproven, stupid attitudes)* they hold sacred; the fewer facts they know. They are also ready to die to preserve those beliefs *(potential lies)*. As people move upward on the ladder of evolution, truth and knowledge gain in prestige and respect. However, So far, truth and knowledge are still low on the totem pole—even among the advanced civilizations on earth.

Some backward Indian tribes in Central and South America kill all recently born white-skinned mutant children and twins in their respective tribes, saying that such children come from Hell. *The Laws of Manu*, a type of Hindu code of conduct, state that farmers are hell-bound because they kill small animals and insects while plowing their fields. In certain cultures, people believe *(demonstrate their stupidity publicly)* that dinner guests must show their appreciation for well-prepared meals by belching loudly. If we, here in the United States, did this, we'd become ostracized socially. Christians are convinced that Jesus Christ was a Jew. The Moslems will insist that he was an Arab.

We can't always depend on our feelings to tell us what is best for us. In the late 40s, When I was a college student in Mexico, I fell deeply in love with a *señorita* lovelier than any Barbie doll. At first, she returned my affection. However, an older man came along, convincing her to marry him instead of me. For more than twenty-five years afterwards, even though I had since married and raised a family, I mourned the loss of that first love. After all those years of mourning, I returned to Mexico City to visit her family, with whom I had never lost contact. At a wedding reception, I saw this woman who had "caused" me two decades and a half of grief. Though she was only 45 years old, she appeared to be seventy. Nearly toothless, she was disgustingly obese. Her head appeared to be attached directly to her shoulders, seemingly without a neck, and looking like an egg perched atop an upright watermelon. "Eeek!" I screamed inwardly. "Did I spend nearly a generation mourning the loss of *that*? By tossing me into the wastebasket, that lady did me a favor for which I'll be forever grateful!"

Though I was 47 years old at the time, I represented thirty-seven. Noting this, the lady told her sisters that she repented having jilted me for an older man. She now realized that I would have been better for her. I told the sisters that I had "forgiven" her. "Everything happened for the best," I thought; "—my best!"

Needless to say, I never pined for her again. But think of all the years I spent suffering the loss of a love that was never more than a mirage. Should we human beings spend more time studying what love is all about instead of letting ignorance rule our feelings?

Most attitudes about human morality and behavior are changing constantly, just as I once adored my first love and then changed my feelings later on. When I was a child back in El Dorado, Kansas, during the 30s and 40s, some people thought that sex was an unholy sin that should be overcome by any means possible. Mom and Dad belonged to the Nazarene church, a fundamentalist Christian sect. The pastor often preached that couples should have sexual relationships only when they wanted children. His unhappy wife, whose tortured countenance never failed to advertise her inner frustrations, told the women in the congregation that this man practiced what he preached. But not always. I could have told her that one night, I caught this saintly pastor and a married choir singer kissing each other passionately. A Mennonite friend of Mom and Dad became so disgusted by his priapic impulses that he castrated himself.

After entering puberty, I noted that I was unable to keep my sexual desires hermetically sealed. I was constantly on the prowl. Dad even convinced me that I was some sort of sexual pervert. He said that "God" bestowed sexual desires on humans only after they got themselves chained and enslaved for life in front of a preacher's pulpit. The decent girls in town wouldn't come close to me—and perhaps that was a blessing. Since few of the local girls would have me, I didn't marry before age 20 as most of my classmates did. Fifty years later, when my wife and I were attending a neighborhood reunion, some of those same girls who had avoided me in "the good old days," said, "Gene, do you remember when we girls rejected you for being sexually promiscuous? We'd now reject you if you were not!"

We're all told that military training and team sports build character. How can people continue to believe that lie? Many soldiers are well disciplined only on their respective bases. They often turn into Africanized bees in the towns off base. Fights and even killings are almost commonplace during and after major team sport events. Yet, hardly anyone turns from Dr. Jekyll into Mr. Hyde during and after tiddliwinks, chess, tennis and golf matches.

The religions brainwash us to think that they teach "enduring, eternal values" to their followers. If they're correct, why does every generation reinterpret "eternal values" differently? Why is it that different religious and political beliefs *(self- and collective destructive attitudes)* are the major causes of nearly all wars?"

The different beliefs *(weird or unverifiable convictions)* in this world are nearly as infinite as the sands covering our beaches. And, like the in and out movement of tides, they are constantly moving about and changing.

Because beliefs *(the sweethearts of fools)* are hardly ever based on truths, certain knowledge, and valid premises, why has mankind enthroned them as being even greater than demonstrable facts and knowledge? Man has made the gross mistake of convincing himself that human behavior may not have to conform to any kind of physical or natural laws. This anomaly we'll explore thoroughly in the rest of this book. We'll dissect several kinds of beliefs *(potentially invalid self-delusion)* surgically, both individual and collective, beginning with their origins, up to the present age. At the same time, I will present a simple antidote to the disease of belief *(the world's oldest and most effective method of worshiping foolishness)*, which all human beings of every religious persuasion and culture will find acceptable—except those who have always capitalized handsomely from this human infirmity. If mankind will interpret and define all the words related to belief *(willful deceit)* exactly as the dictionaries present them, I can **guarantee**: nearly all wars and contention in this world will either come to an end or become dramatically defanged. Geniuses will multiply like rabbits. Human progress will become dramatically accelerated. Millennium 2000 will then, indeed, usher in a New Age—as we were always taught in the preceding one.

Chapter X

The Genesis and History of Human Belief Systems

Belief *(a way of enforcing lies by force)* is one of the most primitive of animal instinctual awareness mechanisms, alongside the primal urges for food, water, sex, shelter, and the like. In the beginning of human existence, beliefs *(primitive guesswork)* helped early Man create strategies for survival and group cohesion. Whenever early Man confronted a problem or danger that he could not handle by just fighting or fleeing, he created an untested strategy, hoping desperately that it would help him survive. For example, like some bird species, one of the first humans could have pretended to be wounded, limping just beyond his enemies long enough to lead them to some friends lying in wait behind a large rock. If the enemy fell for the deceit he was saved. If the enemy did not, he was doomed, along with his companions. Even then, beliefs *(the world's most sought-after badges of ignorance)* guaranteed nothing. In this modern Age of Knowledge, *they guarantee even less!*

Some early strategists were cleverer than others. The members of their respective tribes accepted their leadership, just as towns in the early West employed certain gun-handy individuals as town marshals. Man tends to be a herd animal. Being weak physically and with no natural armaments, such as long teeth, sharp claws or armor-like hide, early Man learned hundreds of thousands of years ago that he could survive only by living with and within a group. To enjoy the safety and combined strength of the group, each individual had to demonstrate blind loyalty to the leaders, obeying all their commands and accepting a particular level in the tribe's pecking order. Individualists were driven from the tribe and forced to survive all by themselves.

Occasionally, some leaders made fatal mistakes in judgement, resulting in the loss of lives or ineffectiveness in the chase. Let's suppose that a certain tribe was driven out of its mountain stronghold and forced to survive on open, flat plains. The techniques used for surviving in a mountainous environment became unworkable on the plains. If the leader could not adapt adequately to different environments and situations, others challenged his ability to lead.

As humans began to learn successful survival strategies applicable to many types of situations and food-acquiring territories, combining and permuting them in various ways, they became more and more creative and effective. At this time, mankind began to develop the ability to think more rationally. However, in those insecure days, when people rarely roamed more than ten or twenty miles from their home territories, certain tribal members objected to innovators, saying, "If it ain't broken, don't fix it." The community then started pressuring the innovators to follow the established norms—or leave the tribe. From time to time, the leading innovators obtained followers who aided them in fighting those tribal members supporting the established norms for developing survival strategies.

Occasionally, some potential innovators began to think about strategies for handling seemingly impossible problems, such as droughts, the disappearance of their preferred animal food, excessive rains, storms, and other situations. Being abysmally ignorant, with not even the concept of scientific approaches to the problems of life, they decided that certain invisible beings brought rain, made the sun shine, and performed other tasks beyond mankind's ability. What we now call Nature, they called "gods"—or just plain "God." One man probably reasoned that if a person sacrificed newly born infants on stone altars, and at certain times of the year, the "rain gods" would pour water down from the skies. Convinced that these sacrifices were valid, many people joined his rain-oriented sacrificial cult. Perhaps another man reasoned that special dances would bring rain. He, too, organized a following of "true believers *(devoted fools)*." Sometimes the different rain cults declared war on each other because each thought that its respective cult was "the only sure way to attract rain to the earth."

For thousands of years, all races and nations have "believed" *(imagined)* that each human has a physical and an ethereal body. Supposedly, the physical body turns into earth at certain intervals called "death," leaving an undying ethereal body without a material sheath. Because the idea *(unproven suspicion)* that Man is both physical and ethereal has existed since his remotest beginnings, I truly "believe" *(don't have any valid and acceptable proofs to defend my thesis)* that Man at one time had an intimate knowledge of the reality of ethereal beings. But should I try to force other people to accept my own realities? Don't forget this: *Even though I personally have solid proof to support my convictions, if I can't prove them valid to others, such as showing them ghosts, and the like, my knowledge is still "belief." I have no right to convert or convince anyone. A "True Believer" and the "solitary knower" deserve to be stuffed in the same basket.*

So far as we know, all religions derive from the ancient Kubera *(Kheeber or Hebrew)* and *Shiva* cults of Northwestern India. Kubera, whom Hindu mythology treats as a God-man, was supposedly the first individual to mine, smelt, refine, mold and smith gold, silver, copper, iron, and other metals. Kubera was probably a tribe that discovered the art of mining and metal-working, for the Hebrew word *Kheever (Hebrew)* means "association or group." Another ancient king, *Shiva, Siva, Yishvara* or *Isvara,* allied his kingdom with that of the Kuberas. Eventually, he became both the *seen—unseen* aspect of Nature. Cappeller's online dictionary of Sanskrit states that Kubera and Shiva were the same person. For the Jews, Shiva has become *Yeshua, Tseva,*

Yahve, Jahve, or *Jehovah.* The Christian word for both the material and non-material aspects of Nature is *Yeshua* or *Jesus.*

According to the remotest followers of the Kubera-Shiva cults, people and leaders known for their goodness and willingness to improve Man's lot on earth became guardian angels after leaving the physical sheath. They were called *Yakhus* or *Yaksas.* Even in modern Orthodox Judaism, wealthy, highly educated, and philanthropically oriented Jews are called *Yakhsan* having *Yeekhoos/Yichus*

In times of need and danger, the ancient Hindus pleaded for the intervention of Yakhus or Yaksas. Eventually, the most popular Yakhus or Yaksas became gods. True to their original humanity, some "gods" were supposed to be more effective than others. Different cults sprang up, dedicated to the most popular "gods" and the most reliable rituals and disciplines for attracting their favor. Each city had its own deities. Naturally, not being scientific, each group "believed" *(depended on unproven ideas)* that its religious philosophy was the Only Way. And each group was more than enthusiastic about defending its particular deities and views "to the death!"

Century by century, beliefs *(wrong, fixed obsessive ideas)* began to give way to valid concepts of what Nature is all about. But valid knowledge is still a 97 pound weakling when compared to the beliefs *(unproven ideas)* continuing to hold sway over the mind of Man. Although we like to pound our chests and brag of our accomplishments, true knowledge of Nature is just a single miniscule grain of sand, compared to the fiercely competing totality of belief systems *(collective and self deceptions)* on earth. A survey in 2001 revealed that although 88 percent of Americans feel a connection to the natural world, more than half of the adults surveyed didn't know that the Earth revolves around the sun; 42 percent said they thought early humans lived side by side with dinosaurs. Yet, what we call "Nature" is the "real God" of mankind; not the myriad beliefs *(mental shit)* keeping all humans bound in the chains of ignorance. Furthermore, these "true believers *(people who are proud of their stupidity)*" would rather destroy all mankind and the universe itself, if possible, then admit that "Nature" rules above all. Yet, even though our perceptions of divinity are still lying at the bottom of human perception, doesn't mean that we should be atheists. We should support scientific studies directed toward proving the eternity of life.

During the 19th and 20th centuries, it became apparent that belief *(guesswork)* systems and scientific inquiry were becoming unfriendly competitors. Humans all over the globe became confused and frightened when they saw their "divine concepts" and "gods" being challenged and destroyed. Writers and dramatists began to portray scientists as insane demons bent on destroying the world. The fictional Baron Von Frankenstein and the monster he created from assorted parts of human cadavers personified many individuals' stereotypical image of scientists. Religious people especially feared Darwin and his theory of evolution, which listed human beings as hairless chimpanzees. Even now, Orthodox Jews, the Christian Religious Right, the Moslems and many Hindus are hostile to the theory of evolution, but they don't complain excessively about taking advantage of the tremendous medical advances that have sprouted from evolution science. Certain states in the American union have passed laws limiting the freedom of teachers to teach evolution in the schools. However, the overwhelming evidence that evolution is a scientific reality has made it impossible to enforce those laws. After the teachers get their orders to either quit or tone down the teaching of evolutionary science, they just go back to their respective classrooms and continue where they left off.

In the early 1950s, an ex-dock worker and brilliant thinker, Eric Hoffer, published a book showing how belief systems and their adherents were becoming increasingly anachronistic in this modern, scientifically progressive world: *The True Believer.* Although I was in my 20s at the time, Hoffer's book captured my soul.

Long before reading that book, I had already concluded that belief systems *(strategies to hoodwink fools)* sapped the strength out of all human beings. Groaning from the tight restrictions on human thought processes, imposed on me in the small Bible-belt town of El Dorado, Kansas, where I was born and raised, I decided to go to college in Mexico and learn other points of view. I was shocked and disappointed to discover that the Mexicans were even more addicted to mind-eroding beliefs *(voluntary destruction of the mind)* than the *gringos* were. They told me that firm, unshakable beliefs *(stubborn, fanatical love for ignorance)* were the measures of great men. Having always been ambivalent about my own beliefs *(personal choices of stupid attitudes)*, more than willing to change them when the need arose, I began to feel mentally inadequate. Later on, after traveling and living in other countries, learning about their respective belief systems *(superstitions)*, my fellow Kansans' tight, compressed beliefs *(ridiculous guessing games)* and attitudes began to seem like that "crazy kid stuff," when compared to the mental ordure *(beliefs)* that people of other cultures peed into their brains!

Hoffer's book concentrated mainly on the collective aspects of the mentally damaging effects of belief *(strategies of choosing to remain ignorant)* systems. He did not realize at the time that belief *(nutburger)* systems are the underlying cause of most forms of individual backwardness and stupidity. If you want to measure a person's degree of mental efficiency, measure his beliefs *(voluntary throat-cutting)* and attitudes against his knowledge and willingness to learn new and/or valid concepts. If a person's mental faculties are not congenitally retarded—or damaged, as in unfortunate accidents, each individual has the mental capacity to become a genius. Only his beliefs *(personal determination to advertise his stupidity to the world)* and attitudes keep him in chains.

Hoffer's brilliant exposé of the villainy caused by *true beliefs (false premises)* became the talk of the entire world. For a while, his publishers could not print books fast enough. But the human addiction to enthroning beliefs *(love of ignorance)* over truth won the day—or should I say, *the ages to come*? Poor Eric would roll over in his grave if he knew that he is now the guru-messiah of another cult of *true believers* who are enemies of non-Hofferite *true believers!* Here we are again—*back where we started from.*

The following are some of Hoffer's aphorisms pertaining to the message I want to convey in this book:

> The only way to predict the future is to have power to shape the future. Those in possession of absolute power can not only prophesy and make their prophesies come true, but they can also lie and make their lies come true.

> We can be absolutely certain only about things we do not understand.

> An empty head is not really empty; it is stuffed with rubbish. Hence the difficulty of forcing anything in to an empty head.

> The capacity for getting along with our neighbor depends to a large extent on the capacity for getting along with ourselves. The self-respecting individual will try to be as tolerant of his neighbor's shortcomings as he is of his own.

> Passionate hatred can give meaning and purpose to an empty life. Thus people haunted by the purposelessness of their lives try to find a new content not only by dedicating themselves to a holy cause but also by nursing a fanatical grievance. A mass movement offers them unlimited opportunities for both.

> There is apparently some connection between dissatisfaction with oneself and proneness to credulity. The urge to escape our real self is also an urge to escape the rational and the obvious. The refusal to see ourselves as we are develops a distaste for facts and cold logic. There is no hope for the frustrated in the actual and the possible. Salvation can come to them only from the miraculous, which seeps through a crack in the iron wall of inexorable reality. They asked to be deceived.

The uncompromising attitude is more indicative of an inner uncertainty than a deep conviction. The implacable stand is directed more against the doubt within than the assailant without.

Animals can learn, but it is not by learning that they become dogs, cats, or horses. Only man has to learn to become what he is supposed to be.

Unity and self-sacrifice, of themselves, even when fostered by the most noble means, produce a facility for hating. Even when men league themselves mightily together to promote tolerance and peace on earth, they are likely to be violently intolerant toward those not of a like mind.

The truth seems to be that propaganda on its own cannot force its way into unwilling minds; neither can it inculcate something wholly new; nor can it keep people persuaded once they have ceased to believe. It penetrates into minds already open, and rather than instill opinion it articulates and justifies opinions already present in the minds of its recipients.

To most of us nothing is so invisible as an unpleasant truth. Though it is held before our eyes, pushed under our noses, rammed down our throats—we know it not.

The untalented are more at ease in a society that gives them valid alibis for not achieving than in one where opportunities are abundant. In an affluent society, the alienated who clamor for power are largely untalented people who cannot make use of the unprecedented opportunities for self-realization, and cannot escape the confrontation with an ineffectual self.

There are many who find a good alibi far more attractive than an achievement. For an achievement does not settle anything permanently. We still have to prove our worth anew each day:

we have to prove that we are as good today as we were yesterday. But when we have a valid alibi for not achieving anything we are fixed, so to speak, for life. Moreover, when we have an alibi for not writing a book, painting a picture, and so on, we have an alibi for not writing the greatest book and not painting the greatest picture. Small wonder that the effort expended and the punishment endured in obtaining a good alibi often exceed the effort and grief requisite for the attainment of a most marked achievement.

Propaganda does not deceive people; it merely helps them to deceive themselves.

There are many who find the burdens, the anxiety, and the isolation of an individual existence unbearable. This is particularly true when the opportunities for self-advancement are relatively meager, and one's individual interests and prospects do not seem worth living for. Such persons sooner or later turn their backs on an individual existence and strive to acquire a sense of worth and a purpose by an identification with a holy cause, a leader, or a movement. The faith and pride they derive from such an identification serve them as substitutes for the unattainable self-confidence and self-respect.

Far more crucial than what we know or do not know is what we do not want to know. One often obtains a clue to a person's nature by discovering the reasons for his or her imperviousness to certain impressions.

All leaders strive to turn their followers into children.

The frustrated follow a leader less because of their faith that he is leading them to a promised land than because of their immediate feeling that he is leading them away from their unwanted selves. Surrender to a leader is not a means to an end but a ful-fillment. Whither they are led is of secondary importance.

The ability to get along without an exceptional leader is the mark of social vigor.

When watching men of power in action it must be always kept in mind that, whether they know it or not, their main purpose is the elimination or neutralization of the independent indi-vidual the independent voter, consumer, worker, owner, thinker and that every device they employ aims at turning men into a manipulable "animated instrument" which is Aristotle's definition of a slave.

We have rudiments of reverence for the human body, but we consider as nothing the rape of the human mind.

The rule seems to be that those who find no difficulty in deceiving themselves are easily deceived by others. They are easily persuaded and led.

A doctrine insulates the devout not only against the realities around them but also *against* their own selves. The fanatical believer is not conscious of his envy, malice, pettiness and dis-honesty. There is a wall of words between his consciousness and his real self.

We lie loudest when we lie to ourselves.

Chapter XI

How People React to Truth and Belief

While you are reading this chapter, you may become tempted, as elsewhere in this book, to complain that I am giving too many repetitions of the obvious. However, I need to make these repetitions to enlighten my readers sufficiently to understand that we humans have been brainwashed to disregard the obvious. Hopefully, by the time you finish this chapter, your mental vision will be sufficiently awakened to be fully aware that Belief *(willy-nilly guessing)*, as we understand the term, and Truth can no longer co-exist as equals deserving of respect in this Age of Science.

Again, I present the dictionary definition of belief:

> *...an opinion or conviction...confidence in the truth of existence of something not immediately susceptible to rigorous proof...conclusion, persuasion, assurance...Acceptance of or confidence in, an alleged fact or body of facts as true or right without positive knowledge or proof; certainty or unquestioning belief and positiveness in one's own mind that something is true; conviction or settled, profound, or earnest belief that something is right; doctrine; dogma, etc,*

I am assuming that everyone, regardless of his degree or lack of education, religious or not, politically active or not, is more or less in total agreement that these dictionary definitions are fundamentally accurate.

If someone were to start acting like a fanatic, screaming and ranting to you that all dictionaries give an incorrect definition of belief *(self-imposed idiocy)*, how would you react emotionally?

I know without asking that you would regard such a person as either a lunatic or a clown. You would back away from him or have a good laugh. Why would the fanatic's ranting and raving about the incorrectness of dictionary definitions of belief *(stupidity enforced by muscle and potential violence)* not cause you to react negatively? Answer this question if you can.

Thousands of human beings still believe *(make public asses of themselves)* that the earth is flat. In fact, there is even an organization of educated people, dedicated to preserve this notion: The Flat Earth Society. Why does no one get "fighting mad" when the Flat Earth folks express their beliefs *(ignorance)* publicly? Is it possible that Truth does not generally inspire negative feelings and emotions?

Suppose a fanatic screams that you are wrong in thinking that when a person turns on a TV set, certain laws of physics cause its circuit to bring up an image on the screen. "Repent for having believed such devil-spawned lies! Accept my teaching that certain angels descended from Planet Jupiter are causing the screen to produce images!"

Would you get angry and scream back at him? Again, you would either enjoy a good belly laugh or wonder about the mental stability of this clown.

How do you react to this statement: "The sun does not shine. It does not radiate light. The moon does not reflect the light of the sun." Obviously I am negating facts you know to be true. Why don't you get angry and defend your "right" to know that the sun shines and that the moon reflects the sun's light to earth?

If a hard rain started falling upon you, and an acquaintance tried to convince you that it was really a hot, dry, dust storm, could you be converted to his ideas? Would you get angry and tell him that he was a demoniacal heretic?

How would you react if someone told you that you are a son-of-a-bitch? In this case, you might get angry and even violent. Why does being called "son-of-a-bitch" inspire hate and anger in the victims of verbal abuse? A "bitch" is a female dog, not a female human. A human mother is not a dog. So why does such a lie make people angry? The answer: People naturally react negatively to insults, threats, and attacks, whether verbal or physical, even if they aren't real.

Once, when my wife and I were entering a grocery store, two women stopped us, pushed some leaflets in our hands, and began to lecture us on the blessings we would receive if we joined their particular fundamentalist Christian sect. "Salvation is possible only through our organization. We guarantee it."

I said, "There are an estimated 24,000 Christian sects on earth. The members of each sect make the same claims you do. Out of all those 24,000 sects, which one preaches the real truth?"

One of the women answered confidently, "Naturally, ours!"

Have you ever noticed that whenever anyone challenges your most cherished religious and political beliefs *(concrete, scientific proofs that you're stupid and ignorant)*, you have to struggle to refrain from expressing your anger physically? Unlike truths, Beliefs *(the chattering of monkeys)* need constant reinforcement and feeding in order to stay alive. Because they cannot—and will not—prove the validity of their beliefs *(drunken puke)*, true believers *(outrageously overbearing and aggressive guessers)* must constantly keep their views reinforced by any means possible.

When Belief *(Mind vomit)* merges with Truth, the "believer's" *(donkey butt's)* struggle to keep his ideas on the "truth" side even affects his health. Blood pressure and muscle tension increase. Heart rate increases. In many cases, the "Believer" *(champion asshole)* even begins to tremble. It seems that Nature itself is against the union of Belief *(mind puss)* and Truth.

A number of years ago, some prominent speakers and writers announced that God was dead. Immediately, America's religious communities howled in pain, demanding the blood of those infidels who had spread such a dastardly lie. It did not occur to them that if they

really *knew* that God exists, they wouldn't have needed to react negatively to such announcements. Truth and knowledge don't inflame
human passions. By reacting passionately to detractors, the religious
communities reveal their own fears and doubts. They probably think as
one of my Mexican girl friends did. One day, She asked, "Gene, what do
you think about my Mexico?"

I answered, "Exactly what you think."

Screaming in rage, the girl started pounding me with her fists. "How
dare you insult my native land!"

Beliefs *(mind shit)* are actually mental hallucinations of imaginary
animal territories. To make these hallucinations seem real, true believers *(self-confessed con-men)* must strike out at anyone threatening to
pull them back into reality; they may force their adversaries to join
them by force and by various other devilish pressures, as when Islam
evangelized people at sword point in 500 A.D. The history of human
beliefs *(voluntary submission to the king of fools)* has left nothing but a
trail of blood and broken lives, from earliest times to the present day.

During the Catholic Inquisition, even scientists were burned at the
stake for uttering truths that are commonly known and accepted today.

When I was a young college student in Mexico, I read a booklet criti-
cizing the Jews for having told "horrible lies" about how the Church persecuted them during the Inquisition. Although I no longer have that
booklet in my possession, I'll never forget the gist of what it said: "Those
intolerant Jews accuse us of tying them to stakes and burning them alive
in front of the churches. They are demoniacal liars. They were burned
alive within the churches themselves, during special religious services in
which choruses of nuns sang about merciful God; while they were burning, the holy fathers prayed for their redemption in the afterlife!"

Suppose the condemned Spanish Jews had lied about where and why they
were burned alive. As far as I'm concerned, burning people alive is a barbaric,
inhumane act, either in or out of church. I'm certain that the Jews roasted
alive by the Inquisition would have concurred with me on this point.

People can become so hypnotized by belief *(delusional)* systems that they will give up their lives without a complaint. The followers of David Koresh's Waco, Texas followers allowed themselves to be burned alive in their headquarters, rather than surrender to government authorities. No one can ever forget the Jim Jones tragedy in Guyana some years ago when he and his followers all committed suicide *enmasse.*

Every imaginable sort of strategy is used in order to get people to conform to certain beliefs *(willingness to sell their souls to devils)* : murder, violence, threats, social pressures, mockery, name-calling, bribery, and the like. When I was living in Latin America, I noticed that the missionaries gave prospective converts free food and medical services, just to pull them into the fold. Then, after they converted, they had to provide for their own food and medical treatment. Some years ago, a radical Christian sect offered men sex in exchange for their minds.

As the advances in science permeate every aspect of human life, human belief *(blind leading the blind)* systems find themselves pushed farther toward the brink of extinction. In their last moments, they may wreak unimaginable wrath and destruction on Earth before evaporating into nothingness. I hope that what I say in this book will prevent such a holocaust.

I always tremble when powerful economic factions and political groups from different countries get together to decide what is best for the world. If I were one of these delegates, I'd be more than ashamed to attend meetings in which Man's lowest and most despicable animal awareness system is glorified and allowed to decide the fate of mankind!

Nobody can be around me for more than thirty minutes without finding out that I have a deep and abiding admiration for Latin Americans. I am even a *wannabe.* Yet, I am not so blind that I can't see how their "political beliefs" keep them from advancing. They believe *(delude themselves)* that they can get political stability and economic-social viability only with the help of charismatic revolutionaries and leaders, idealism, political systems like Marxism, and the like—or fleeing to the United States. Year after year, generation after generation, they fall into the same trap. In their opinion, if they keep on playing Russian roulette over and over again, eventually the hammer of their political pistol will click on an empty chamber—and they'll be saved. I have never been able to convince them—and possibly never will—that systems and beliefs *(voluntary mental suicide)* are mirages. They'll never work over the long run. By robbing the rich and giving to the poor, as they'd like to do, they just produce more poverty and suffering.

The only way that mankind is ever going to solve the problem of need and oppression is to create more wealth—not to divide the wealth that exists or make laws limiting the freedom of entrepreneurs. For the first time in human history, mankind has the magic wand for making every person on earth wealthy and those who are already rich wealthier: genetic engineering, nanotechnology, robotics, alternative energies, and the like. These new developments alone may make everyone in the world wealthy, eliminate poverty, end backbreaking labor forever, increase the human life span, and protect the environment.

No Karl Marx, Vladimir Lenin, Fidel Castro or Che Guevara will ever bring happiness and prosperity to anyone—only the world's scientists.

Eric Hoffer wrote principally about the damage that "True Believing" *(cramming one's bodily wastes into other people's brains)* does to humans collectively. However, people can believe *(put a mental pistol to their heads)* destructive, unjust things about themselves, such as being unworthy, unintelligent, ugly, racially inferior, unloved, etc. Furthermore, a person's negative beliefs *(mind vomit)* about himself need not emanate from the group to which he belongs. More often than not, people voluntarily choose to force limitations upon themselves.

A person whose mind has accepted a destructive belief *(willingness to cut his brain out of his cranial cavity)* can even will it to manifest itself on or in his body. During the 1940s, when I was working on the Santa Fe railroad, my friends and I convinced a young boy from the Arkansas hills that we had placed some croton oil, a super-powerful purgative, in one of his sandwiches. A few hours later, the boy developed such a powerful case of diarrhea that he had to go to the hospital.

Mexico is another country that has allowed itself to become enslaved by beliefs *(self-imposed barbarism)*. And don't forget: a good belief *(willingness to be a fool)* or non-belief *(willingness to be a fool)* can be just as potentially destructive as a bad one. Many millions of Mexicans have convinced themselves that their country is poor. This belief *(stupidity)* is called *malinchismo.* Malina was a young non-Aztec princess from what is now the Mexican State of Vera Cruz, who helped the Spaniards conquer the Aztecs. Therefore, anyone who thinks *(deludes himself)* he has a better future out of Mexico, or who has convinced himself that foreign products are better than those manufactured in Mexico, is a *malinchista.*

The truth is that Mexico is extremely rich in human and natural resources. If the Mexicans continue to rely on beliefs *(abhorrence of truth)*, scorning science and verifiable truths, it will never progress satisfactorily. A famous Mexican scientist, Juan Enríques Cabot, stated in an interview with the Mexican magazine *Muy Interesante:* "The fundamental problem in Mexico is that we don't give enough attention to science…If our heads of government…continue to scorn this country's finest minds and neglect the well-being of Mexico's people, this economy will not grow." (May 2001; pp. 37-38.)

My first wife, a Central American, taught my two children that foxes were skunks. Whenever they did not take their daily baths, she would say to them, "You smell like a fox." I thought that her confusion about the difference between foxes and skunks was hilarious—even cute. I said to myself, "I'm going to let my children find out the difference on their own." That was a serious mistake on my part. In this New Age of Knowledge, wherever and whenever possible, beliefs *(voluntary insanity)* must be corrected as quickly as possible.

One day, while my son and I were out taking a stroll, a young man passed us, holding a baby fox in his arms. My son said, "Look, Dad, that man is carrying a strange-looking little dog."

I answered, "Son, that's a fox."

"But dad, foxes are black with white stripes running down their backs; they stink."

"Son, it's time to tell you that those animals are skunks."

My son told me that he became traumatized upon learning that foxes were not skunks.

If given time to take root, beliefs *(hate for truth)* always traumatize, stupefy, confuse, and pervert the human mind, even destroying the body. In no way do great men believe *(become public clowns)*. They know!

Chapter XII

The Real Meaning of Idol Worship

Hindus often get defensive when Christians criticize them for having multiple gods and idols. A number of Hindu apologists have written books defending idol worship. Actually, none of those books would probably have ever been written had they not been themselves as ignorant of what "idol worship" means as the Christians are. I don't blame the Hindus for lashing out at what they correctly know to be Christian hypocrisy, for the Christians, unwilling to face their own hypocrisy, openly worship more gods than the Hindus do. Although the Hindus recognize the existence of millions of deities, they actually worship only 33. At last count, there are 24,000 Christian cults in the world. These Christian cults exist because their respective founders created their own unique ideas about Jesus Christ, his personality, and the God from which he emanated. In this respect, Hinduism is no different from Christianity, for each of their idols now represents one aspect of the Godhead, but this was not true at one time. The Hindu "gods" were once men like ourselves. Historian Sumit Mishra states in his website, *http://www.indusscript.net/history.htm:*

> We have been led to believe that the vedic deities are the representations of the different aspects of the nature. That may be true in respect of certain abstract deities or those derived from the typically vedic roots at the inflexional stage. But the vedic words of the agglutinative origin or those compressed from the isolating stage may be representing the typical

human beings of the society. All the qualities of the gods make them typical human beings with special uniforms, discharging various duties of the society. It is difficult to see those aspects of the vedic gods in history.

The officials of the Indus society were human beings; they were treated as gods in the Vedic Society.

The Christians received nearly all their spiritual words from Northern India, but the followers of Jesus have changed their meaning far beyond what they were originally intended to convey. *Idolatry,* derived from the Proto-Indo-European (PIE) languages, was originally *A-Dol-Taur,* or the human weakness for making unreal symbols and interpretations of what the forces of Nature are all about. Graven images are just one tiny aspect of idolatry. The ancients taught that Nature is Creation, The Primal Vulva, or The Eternal Beginning *(God; Khod; Khoda, etc.).* The physical aspect of Nature or Creation *(God)* is *Yishvara, Isvara, Yesh, etc.* We call it *Yeshua, Isa,* or *Jesus.* According to the ancients, Man's purpose on earth was to unlock the secrets of Nature and continue the Eternal Birth of the Universe, emanating always from The Primal Vulva ("The Big Bang" or God). Over the millenniums, God lost its connotation of "Eternal Rebirth" and became the "Supreme Deity."

The ancients further preached that all misinterpretations of any aspect of Nature created "idols" *(the modern understanding of beliefs)* or conditions that would damage and even destroy mankind's life and happiness on earth. Here are some aspects of "idol worship" *(beliefs as Modern Man understands the term).* Let's suppose that Nature intended for Man to someday learn how to induce low-pressure systems in certain areas and bring rain. However, some men decided that only special chants, sacrifices, and rituals would attract the favor of "The Rain God." Naturally, chants, sacrifices, and rituals do not bring about low-pressure systems. As a result, Man finds himself still faced with the problem of bringing rain to certain areas.

Let's suppose that a group of people have decided that by believing *(becoming insane)* in, praying to and worshiping a human or animal representation of a certain aspect of Nature, a person can bring about unique manifestations of Nature, such as the cure of some diseases. If this approach to Nature does not "compute," the humans involved in this insanity *(believing)* ultimately bring down more disease and suffering upon themselves.

At the time of this writing, the secular and religious communities are squaring off against each other on the subject of human embryonic research and experimentation. The scientists have discovered that substances in the human embryo can be used to revolutionize medicine, turning it from a "practice" or "art" into a true science. The Christian and non-Christian communities tend to oppose such research on the grounds that an "embryo" is a tiny "human" and that destroying one is like killing a human. The *truth* is that a "human" is that being who has the fully developed nervous system of a human. The difference between the nervous system of an embryo and that of a human is as different, if not more so, than the nervous system of a one celled organism and that of a highly evolved human, such as a person like Albert Einstein. But many religious communities will not accept that this truth. By so doing, they are delaying the progress of medicine and condemning millions of *real human beings* to a life of unbearable suffering.

Nature gave mankind the ability to use rational thought and develop scientifically valid solutions to all his problems, both physical and spiritual. But scientific investigation requires that we humans spend our time on earth learning, thinking, and experimenting, in order to find out just exactly what Nature demands of us, even in the behavioral sciences: laborious thought, continuing education, time, and experimentation. We humans long ago found out that it's a lot easier to create our own idols *(beliefs)*, both physical and mental, brainwashing ourselves to imagine that we are perceiving certain realities. It's a lot easier to think that something is so-and-so than it is to find out what it *really* is.

Therefore, some individuals invent exotic "spiritual" solutions" to the problems of life, recruiting adherents by any means possible. But such developments as computers, which engender the constant expansion (God) of knowledge, are putting the spiritual leaders and "belief" merchants out of business. From now on, like it or not, want it or not, we must adhere to more rational modalities; everything must be known for what it is; not what we want or believe *(deceive ourselves)* it to be!

Chapter XIII

Retooling Ourselves to Perceive Reality

Of all the other chapters in this book, this one is the most important. He who obeys the following instructions carefully will catapult himself far into the future. The mindset recommended here will put the smallest and weakest nations on at least an equal basis with the leading powers on earth.

Here's the new mindset:

From now on, we humans must remain passionately and forever watchful, to insure that our caveman instincts to believe (choose to be inferior) never again get confused with scientific reality.

How does an idea become a scientific theory? In order to validate an idea, scientists use rigorous methods similar to those of mathematics. So that an idea born out of the human mind can become a generally accepted theory, it must be expressed in one or various hypotheses. Validity MUST be proven experimentally. When the results of such experimentation are satisfactory, they are published so that the scientific community may know about them. Unlike "true believers," the scientists who develop their hypotheses do not twist arms and press the tips of their swords to the throats of those whom they intend to "convert."

The scientists who become interested in the hypotheses they read about in the journals will repeat the experiments described, to see whether they can achieve the same results. If their results match those of the creators of the hypotheses, these hypotheses then get their names changed to "scientific theories." Only in this way can "ideas" and "beliefs" legitimatize themselves. Otherwise, they must remain jailed within the dictionary definitions of beliefs.

Far from limiting his freedom of expression, the person who keeps belief *(mind slop)* from becoming enmeshed in truth will express himself as never before. He'll enjoy greater peace and tranquility because he'll no longer need to clash and remonstrate with people. Basically, all he has to do is keep "beliefs *(mind toilets)*" on their own side of the fence.

We should encourage **unlimited** propagation of ideas and beliefs *(unproven ideas)*; only through expressing our own ideas, and trading them with others, can mankind widen his horizons in life. Occasionally, some ideas that Man creates will contain kernels of truth. At that moment, these ideas quit being "beliefs" and "ideas"—if, and only if, they become workable theories that everyone can prove. They'll immediately jump over the fence to Truth where knowledge engenders peace and harmony.

When a person uses "belief *(pee)*" words in expressing his ideas, such as "guess; think; feel certain; feel sure; am convinced; opine; suspect; and the like, he should say what he wants, where he wants, and when he wants without any fear of being challenged or mocked. After all, *by using "belief" words, he is confessing his ignorance publicly:*

I believe that flying saucers exist. = *In my ignorance and lack of proofs, I have brainwashed myself to think I can authoritatively accept flying saucers and little green space men as possibilities.*

I believe in God. = *I am pretending to accept the reality of something that no one has ever proven.*

I am convinced that so-and-so is guilty of the crime of which he is accused. = *My stupid ignorance and arrogance could put a person in danger of being either executed or imprisoned for a crime he may not have committed.*

I assure you that this second-hand auto is in optimum condition. = *I hope you will be naïve enough to buy this car without being absolutely sure that it is in good condition.*

I believe that President 'So-and-So' is stupid. = *Without giving this president a valid, scientifically prepared I.Q test, I have used my own ignorance and stupidity to determine his intelligence or lack of it.*

A famous female TV evangelist used to roll her eyes toward the back of her head and scream to viewers, "I beLEEEEVE in miracles." She was really saying, *"I'm stupid and ignorant enough to deny that natural processes can often lead to astonishing and positive results."*

Here's a rule we must always obey: *If we cannot prove that our ideas are scientific theories or realities, we must keep them fenced on the "belief" side of the fence.*

If I notice that I can turn on lights by flipping a switch, but no one else can do it, I have no right to say that I know what I'm talking about until everyone else can do it as well. If "faith" can move mountains, and I'm a religious person who preaches that this is so, I must at all times be prepared and willing to stand up before any mountain and will it to move to another site. If I cannot do this, I should not preach that "faith" can move mountains.

As long as a person does not confuse his beliefs *(personal place at the bottom of the barrel of human understanding)* with scientifically validated or naturally obvious truths, we should not get angry with him or intimidate him in any way, unless we have some scientifically valid evidence to straighten up his mental processes. But don't win the argument with "statistics" and "studies." "Statistics" and "studies" can be manipulated. Basically, they are worthless. Let the "believer" rant and rave, as long as he is willing to abide strictly by the dictionary definition of belief *(personal level of being a jungle bunny)*. After all, he's being honest enough to admit publicly that he's an ignorant, stupid oaf. Why should you humiliate him further?

Here's a great method of ridding yourself of the curse of belief. As you well know, belief is so firmly entrenched within human nature that we may never conquer it completely. Therefore, when you're talking with people—and suddenly the Devil tempts you to say, "I believe," give it one of the crazy definitions that I have placed in parenthesis after "believe or belief." Examples: I believe (*fill my mind with mental poop)* that Communism is a great political philosophy. I believe (*advertise my stupidity to the world)* in little green men from Mars. Accept my beliefs (*turn your mind to shit)* about religions and politics; etc.

If you and your associates made fun of that word each time you have fallen into the trap of uttering it, in time, the word "belief" would become a joke, *albeit one in extremely bad taste.* Just imagine what could happen in this world if everyone suddenly stopped taking his beliefs seriously.

We should challenge "true believers (*people who shit in front of crowds)*" only when they start expressing their nonsense (*beliefs)* as existential realities: *"John is a nerd;" "All Armenians belong to the Mafia;" "Raw cabbage will repair damaged livers;" etc.* Then and only then must the "true believers (*mind rapists)*" present scientifically validated evidence to support their claims. However, we must not fall into the trap of judging a true believer (*self-confessed idiot)* or accusing him of preaching false doctrines unless we have scientifically valid information to straighten up such a person's disorderly thinking processes. By judging him, we, too, become "true believers" (*true leeches)*.

The rules for debate, winning arguments, and converting people must also keep "beliefs" (*toilet holes)* and "knowledge" separated by high walls.

"Please join my religion. It's the only way you can be saved."— *Exchange your foolishness, stupidity, and ignorance for mine. Then we can both get lost while traveling in the same direction.*

"Let's have a debate on which political party is better: the democrats or the republicans."—*I've got an idea for a fun contest. Let's see who is the greatest fool and nincompoop—you or I! The one who can prove that he is the more ignorant and silly of the two, wins the debate.*

I agree wholeheartedly with your ideas. It feels good to be in the company of people who think as I do.—*I love people whose ignorance, stupidity, inanity, and insanity match mine!*

"Please don't try to change my deeply held beliefs. Respect them."— *Please let me remain a fool.*

When people are playing catch with their ideas and beliefs *(stupidity, ignorance, and superstitions),* they must be especially careful never to forget that "beliefs" *(stale air in empty skulls)* are always expressions of one's degree of ignorance and stupidity. Don't ever debate with existential expressions of ideas and beliefs *(mind rot)* unless you have the ammunition to prove they are theories.

When delegates and leaders of organizations, governments, and the like get together to discuss their differences and find solutions, the participants have every right to find out from the beginning whether these meetings are going to be belief *(mental shit slinging)* battles or sincere quests for truths. If I were a participant in such encounters, I would inquire of the assembly: "Are we here to make one belief *(sewer slop)* win over the other one—or are we here to reveal truths? If we are here to fight for our beliefs *(competition to be stupid asses),* all we are going to get are temporary solutions, if at all. In that case, I'll want to be dismissed as a participant. However, if we are going to salvage even one truth from this mess, I'll stay."

Here's a mystery I want you to solve: Suppose that the Israelis and the Moslems sit down at the negotiating table. At this meeting, the Israelis prove beyond all doubt that they are the rightful masters of the region. Why should the Moslems then concede without a fight?

Suppose the Moslems proved their point. Why should the Israelis then surrender?

If both sides proved that they have a right to control Israel together—that they descend from the same ancestors—that Israel has been the home for both groups for decades, centuries, and millennia, what are the possibilities for peace?

Never Believe in Yourself!

Self-improvement teachers are famous for encouraging their students to believe *(invent false mental images)* in themselves. But a "belief" *(mental farting)* is a potential lie until it can be turned into a scientific theory. Why should you endanger your future and your psyche by pretending you are such-and-such when there is a better way for you to achieve success? To achieve victory, fall in love with your struggle to succeed. Let's suppose you want to become a famous artist. Love your artistic specialty for its sake alone. Improve your skills constantly. Develop friendships with associates and friends who have some authority in your field of endeavor. They'll help you open the doors leading to the goal you wish to reach. Love for one's struggle to accomplish a certain goal is a much more positive way to achieve success than the nonreality called "belief" *(self-imposed ignorance of your true self)*.

Father Baltasar Gracián, unlike that apostle of positive-thinking, Norman Vincent Peale, was an enemy of positive thinking or the belief *(self-deceit)* that a project would be successful:

> *When you start something, don't raise other people's expectations.* What is highly praised seldom measures up to expectations. Reality never catches up to imagination. It is easy to imagine something is perfect, and difficult to achieve it. Imagination marries desire, and conceives much more than things really are. No matter how excellent something is, it never satisfies our preconceptions. The imagination feels cheated, and excellence leads more often to disappointment

than to admiration. Hope is a great falsifier. Let good judgment bridle her, so that enjoyment will surpass desire. Honorable beginnings should serve to awaken curiosity, not to heighten people's expectations. We are much better off when reality surpasses our expectations, and something turns out better than we thought it would. This rule does not hold true for bad things: when an evil has been exaggerated, its reality makes people applaud. What was feared as ruinous comes to seem tolerable.

Go about all your activities with joy, persistence, and dedication—for themselves alone. Then, whatever the outcome of a project, you'll be able to preserve some semblance of happiness should things not work out as you wanted them to.

Never *Not-Believe* in Yourself.

Not-Belief is just negative belief *(a no-no way of remaining stupid)*. Many times, people fall prey to opinions others have of them. Before they know it, they find themselves voluntarily projecting someone's mental image of them, not the image of what they really are. Fall in love with yourself. Fall in love with your struggle to succeed in certain endeavors. Sooner or later, the truth of what you really are will become manifest in your own being.

Personal Truth Perception

Many times, a person witnesses a crime, sees a missing person, observes an auto wreck, and the like. He is often called on to report what he has witnessed. Naturally, the authorities must give him some degree of credibility *(a long word for "belief" or ignorance)*. However, in some cases, such as when one witnesses a crime, the authorities must use their own discretion in deciding to punish the criminal who committed the crime, for there is a possibility of human error. In itself, circumstantial evidence is insufficient for deciding whether an accused person is guilty or innocent.

Private researchers and ordinary people often make important discoveries on their own. For example, I and many other individuals on earth have received ample evidence that spirit entities exist. However, if our discoveries cannot yet be validated under strict laboratory conditions, we should be strictly regarded as "true believers *(bullshitters)*" only. We may not like to be placed in the category of quacks and guessers, *but our lack of recognition is more than just. I would be truly disappointed if anyone on earth accepts my conviction that ghosts exist just because I or anyone else says so—even if we have personal proof.* By all means possible, belief *(mind rot)* and truth must be kept from merging. This is how wars and many other types of frauds and human evils are leashed upon mankind. It is grossly unfair for people to be brainwashed into meekly accepting information that cannot yet be converted into theories. Until now, the religions and politicians of the world have been free to clutter human minds with impunity. But this type of recklessness and irresponsible freedom is becoming increasingly unacceptable. Sooner or later, the religions are going to have to enter the scientific arena or go out of business.

I truly believe *(lack scientific support and proof for my idea)* that the religions will someday use scientific means to prove that the afterlife is a reality. I have a book written by a French priest, in which he declares that he and some other priests have used electronic means to contact the spirit world. However, until now, no lay scientists have expressed any interest in replicating their experiments. Until that day, the hypothesis developed by those priests must stay on the belief *(garbage)* side of the fence. See my book, *Yishvara 2000—The Hindu Ancestor of Judaism Speaks to This Millennium.*

Avoid Skeptics and Skepticism. Skepticism Is Just a Form of Negative Belief *(using the word "No" in such a way as to confirm that you're an asshole).*

At present, mankind's only line of defense against the imposition of potentially invalid beliefs *(deceitful mind traps)* is *skepticism.* A skeptic is a person who doubts or *disbelieves (proves he's a negative fool)* unproven information. By "disbelieving" (not believing), we counter like with like, for "not believing *(confessing that you're a bum)*" is nothing more, nothing less than negative belief *(confessing publicly that your brain is made of shit).* More often than not, skeptics use the same aggressive tactics that "true believers *(monkey brains)*" do: mockery; belittling; pressures of all kinds, and the like. Also, skeptics rarely counter hypotheses or ideas they oppose with facts and figures. Usually, they leave it up to the "true believer *(potential Hitler)*" to defend his point of view.

Now, I state, and as I have stated elsewhere in this book, all forms of hypotheses, such as beliefs, ideas, opinions, and the like have as much right to exist as validated theories, for in nearly all cases, validated theories grow out of someone's previous ideas and conjectures on certain subjects. The truth is, we need more beliefs *(strange, unproven convictions)*, ideas, opinions, and conjectures in the world, but what we don't need is for anyone to ram them down our throats until they have been converted to consistent and stable theories. Least of all, the person who develops hypotheses and ideas does not need to be mocked and derided, for he is just one side of the coin in Man's eternal search for truth. *Is it not enough for him to admit that he can do no more than "believe" the information he reveals? By doing so, he is yelling publicly, "Honk! Honk! Look at me. I'm a slave to unproven ideas! You, too, can be a fool. Let me convert you."*

Since skeptics are "true not-believers" themselves, they should not look down on their brothers who have positive views about certain ideas. The truth is that there is really no such thing as a totally objective thinker on earth. We may be objective about certain things we know to be true, but what about the things we don't know? All of us have some sort of opinions about things we don't know. Even "indifference" is a neutral opinion.

At the time of this writing, I have become the prey of a known skeptic, a certain professor at the world-famous Marash University, in Melbourne, Australia. I have long claimed that most of our American Indians originated in what are now most of the area between what is now Turkey, down to and including present-day Afghanistan and Pakistan. In no way have I crammed my views down anyone's throat. Like any truly sincere investigator, I played by the rules in presenting my ideas about this matter. I published my findings in the popular online E-Zine, *Viewzone.* At the same time, I published three books, *India Once Ruled the Americas, The Last Atlantis Book You'll Ever Have to Read,* and *From Khyber (Kheeber) Pass to Quivira (Kheevira), NM and Baboquivari, AZ—When India Ruled the World! Viewzone* does not pay its authors. Subscription is free. The magazine is famous for its openness to non-orthodox thinkers and researchers. After reading one of my articles in *Viewzone, Who Was Abraham?,* this professor wrote me, stating that I was using "false cognates." I answered him, stating that I was just stating my views and observations in the article and had no desire to debate with or pressure anyone to accept my views if he didn't want to. I also reminded him that *Viewzone* is an open forum for fringe-culture investigators who take "the road less traveled."

A truly scientifically minded person would have stopped reasoning with me after that. However, this one apparently was a *Skeptic's Witness,* of the type that knocks on doors and sells magazines outside convenience stores. He would not let up on me for one second, but instead stalked me as ardently as Inspector Jaubert, the detective in the novel, *Les Miserables.* Like most adherents of fanatical religions, he was concerned for my "poor, lost soul," wanting me to abandon "18th century concepts of linguistics" and embark upon the "true road" of Millennium 2000 linguists. Over and over, he sent me lengthy E-Mails, repeating essentially the same arguments.

Over and over I told this skeptic professor that I would not fight him verbally about my views. I stated my views in my articles and book, but would push them no further. People voluntarily chose to read my works. I didn't choose for them to do so. Finally, he threatened to attack me publicly if I would not recant. I answered him: "Go ahead and attack me all you want. Perhaps many readers will see me as the 'underdog' and buy my books out of compassion. After all, I do want to sell books—as many as possible."

If this professor disapproved of what I am doing, why did he read every word of every edition of *Viewzone,* including my books? He visited *Viewzone's* website of his own volition. He came to me—not me to him. He was in no way pressured to read and comment on the articles in this magazine. The magazine clearly advertises that it is open to all ideas—the weirder the better. Yet, the editor told me that he gets many hate mails every day from people, each cursing, insulting, and even threatening him and his writers. Many of the people who send these hate mails are faithful readers, as this Australian professor is. These are the kinds of "true believers" who cause all the contention in the world. As long as a person with a hypothesis or an idea goes by the rule book, publishing his findings, and refraining from pressuring people beyond his published findings, he should be respected; not belittled, insulted, and persecuted. Benito Juárez, one of Mexico's greatest presidents, once stated, *"El respecto al derecho ajeno es la paz"* ("Respect for the rights of others is peace.")

The good Australian professor also took issue with me on another book I wrote, *Yishvara 2000—The Hindu Ancestor of Judaism Speaks to This Millennium!* In this book, I also attacked beliefs *(mental rattlsnakes)* twisted to appear as true because hypotheses must always be regarded as guesses until they can become theories. And, like most people, *I, too, have passionate and even obsessive ideas about matters I can't prove—enough to qualify me as a retarded savage.* Therefore, I often expressed my "beliefs" in *Yishvara 2000* as I do in this book: *I believe (don't know what the hell I'm talking about); I believe (am a fool)); I believe (am guessing); I believe (can't give reliable information); I believe (think like a jungle bunny); I believe (have mental diarrhea; I believe (will murder you by any means possible), etc.* The man said I wrote like a hypocrite. He told readers that at one point I told people not to take "beliefs" seriously; in another, I expressed what I "believed." But how could I have done otherwise? How could I say that I "knew" something when I could only guess about what it was? *All of us are inextricably bound to beliefs in different intensities.*

Why It Is "Scientific" to Have a Clear Idea of The Difference Between the Meanings of *Belief* and *Verifiable Truth?*

Nature has made a place in this world for everyone. If she could speak to us in a human voice, she would say, "Speak freely on all subjects. Invent hypotheses of all kinds. Each human must be an idea factory. Nothing is too fanciful. Give free reign to your imaginations. Don't worry whether your ideas are valid or not, foolish or wise. Let this life be filled with infinite ideas. Believe; guess; wonder; opine; suspect; think; dream."

At the same time, she orders us, "Do not force any of your beliefs, ideas, and guesswork on anyone. If your belief or idea can't be validated and made a theory, it must remain just a topic of conversation." Only in this way can peace be maintained in the world. No matter how ridiculous, illogical, good or evil the idea, it cannot harm anyone as long as we keep in mind the true definition of what a belief or a hypothesis is.

Nobody needs to force Truth upon anyone. It is immediately self-evident, just like the rising and setting of the sun. With truth, comes peace. Notice the following chart. On one side are hypothesis or beliefs. On the other side are truths. Notice that as long as each stays on his side of the fence, there is no tension or contention:

My Hypothesis or "Belief" Is:	My Theory or "Truth" is:
The moon is made of green cheese.	The moon is a blob of rock and mineral matter.
Adolph Hitler was a sweet little angel.	Adolph Hitler was an evil man. He proved it.
Rabbit's feet bring good fortune.	Education and wisdom bring good fortune.
Computers are works of the Devil.	Computers can change the world for the best.
Evolution is a lie.	Evolution is a verifiable truth.
Only mentally gifted people can learn mathematics.	Anyone can master mathematics if he makes the effort and is persistent.
The different manifestations of Nature are directed by certain gods.	The different manifestations of Nature conform to certain natural laws.
A straight line is the long mark that one makes by moving a pencil alongside a ruler.	A straight line is the shortest distance between two points.
By keeping my mind riveted on God, I can move mountains.	Only by using special machines and the laws of physics can I move mountains.
The earth is flat.	The earth is a sphere.

Let's suppose that one group of people "believes" *(hallucinates)* all the statements in the first column. Another "knows" the validated information in the right column. The right group does not have to defend what they know. The statements validate themselves; they are axiomatic. Why does the right group not feel hostile to the first group? The first group knows that all it "believes" are either lies or information not yet validated by science. They know that they should not force this invalidated information on anyone else. Therefore, there is no tension or hate between the "belief" and the "truth" groups.

As far as Nature is concerned, each group has an important place to play in her scheme of things. The job of one group is to dream of possibilities. The job of the other is to cull out those possibilities that are workable—those that can be developed into theories. And there is no law stating that we can't belong to both groups simultaneously. *In truth, we all do.*

As long as the first group states clearly that its ideas are not yet vali- dated scientifically, those of us who know better must not mock, contra- dict, or challenge them in any way. It is enough that they admit that they are believing and guessing. There's no need to humiliate and belittle them. I cannot emphasize this enough.

Of course, as we all know, some "imagineers" start getting pushy with their ideas. They want them to be made into theories without the cus- tomary validation. To keep them from overstepping their bounds, the members of the right side must ask the aggressive "imagineers," "Have you forgotten the definition of belief? Review it. What proof do you have in order to treat your ideas as gospel truth or reality?"

If the "imagineer" cannot get his ideas validated, the unwritten law of Nature is, "If you can't prove an idea, keep it in the hypothesis and beliefs column.

Only too often, "imagineers" or "believers" will state their hypotheses in existential terms: *The people in that ethnic group are all thieves. That brand of automobile is carelessly manufactured and built with cheap parts. My political party can save our nation, etc.*

When "believers *(haters of truth)*" insist on the existential reality of their ideas, they must be reined in; they must be compelled to furnish their proofs. For example, perhaps a religious person may say to you, "If you accept my religion, believing in it blindly, you will be able to move mountains and raise the dead upon command."

All thinking people must demand that religious believers in miracles give examples of members of their respective sects, who can perform such divine wonders. If the "believer" will not prove that certain adher- ents to his philosophy can perform miracles, in the same way that we can prove that computers work, or that the sun rises and sets, he must be urged to calm down until he can provide adequate evidence to prove his point. Generally, such individuals will say, "I can do this, but only if you will believe me blindly." Your answer must be something like, "I regard myself as a sane person. I don't want to hallucinate. Hallucinations may get me sent to the 'funny farm.'"

Trouble is always a possibility when "believers" start cannibalizing one another. One side screams, "Is!" The other one answers, "Isn't!" "Is!" "Isn't!" "Isn't so." "Is so." Finally, when they get tired of screaming back and forth, violence may take the place of words. No one on earth is more dangerous than "the true believer."

It is a provable theory; it is a fact of life that "beliefs (*lies*)" can be backed up only by muscle, repression, and group pressures.

During the first week of May, 2001, Pope John Paul went to Greece to seek closer ties between Roman Catholicism and the Greek Orthodox Church. A report about the meeting in the *Los Angeles Times* stated, "Catholics and Orthodox disagree on…whether to use unleavened bread in the Eucharist and to require that priests be celibate and how to interpret the doctrine of the Holy Spirit…."

Of what good was the meeting if neither side could produce a validated theory justifying the superiority of its religious practices over any other? Why is unleavened bread in the Eucharist more spiritually energizing than bread containing yeast? How does celibacy, or lack of it, make one priest better or worse than another? Just what is the Holy Spirit? What are the scientific theories proving its reality?

Can you imagine a meeting between scientific minds in which two groups would bicker over whether electricity is a reality or not? Such a meeting would be unthinkable.

I recently read a Hindu article in which the writer defended the worship of idols and the caste system. He said that people become unhappy in life when they change professions or reeducate themselves in other fields of endeavor. Why did he not give any validated scientific theory to prove his point?

An author of an article about the growth of Islam in the United States stated that the "proof" that God prefers Islam over any other religion is that only the most educated and highly placed Americans are converting. And he did not mention the ignorant Afghan Talibans. How did he get such a message from "God?" Why didn't he tell everyone how to get messages directly from God? Also, what does being educated and highly placed have to do with being more highly spiritual than anyone else? Perhaps such Moslems should think like a gentleman who once said to me, "You have two college degrees. You are even a teacher. Yet, you don't act like one."

I answered, "Hell, man, having a good education does not necessarily indicate I'm not stupid in certain areas. This is America! I have the same right to act stupid at times that you do!"

Many Moslem leaders promise the following benefits to fanatical followers willing to commit suicide in the war against Islam's enemies: eternal life in paradise; permission to see the face of Allah; around-the-clock sexual relations in paradise with 72 young virgins; the guarantee of eternal bliss in heaven to 70 of a prospective martyr's relatives.

Although Christian authorities are fuzzy on what eternal benefits dead Christians can enjoy after passing away, they do promise many mouth-watering fringe benefits, such as streets paved with gold, white clothing that never gets dirty, bird wings, eternal retirement from all kinds of work, reunion with family members, automatic mastery of the harp, and the like. A Jehovah's Witness missionary guaranteed that if I converted, I would enjoy even more sexual partners than those the Moslems offer to prospective suckers.

What religious people must understand is that we who are not active churchgoers require some ironclad guarantees. Let us suppose that a shy man afraid to even talk to women spends all of his life in sexual need. In desperation, he joins a certain offbeat cult to at least assure that he'll satiate his sexual desires in Paradise. Wouldn't he feel somewhat cheated if he blew up his body in a busy Israeli marketplace, only to wake up in "wherever" without even the opportunity to masturbate?

Why can't religious authorities test their hypotheses scientifically? *That's all the people of the world are asking.* After all, the scientists freely offer the rest of us the certainty of TV sets, automobiles, airplanes, microwave ovens, etc. Why don't the religious authorities reveal the sources of their information and the methods of proving that their hypotheses are valid? Why can't the preacher walk over the surface of the fish pond in the church patio without sinking? Why can't he turn three loaves of blood into a thousand? Why can't he bring the dead back to life? Are we "unbelievers" being unreasonable?

Few religious people can distinguish between belief and truth. In their minds, these two diametrically opposite mental attitudes must always be merged. As intelligent and wise as he was, the immortal Jewish thinker Rebbe Menachem Schneerson, one of the greatest of modern philosophers, could not see that trouble befalls mankind when he merges belief and truth:

> For mankind to exist in harmony, we must listen to the voice that Noah heard after the flood. We must accept that there is a set of absolute values set by the Creator of the world, values that cannot be played about with to suit our convenience. Values from beyond the subjective minds of men.

> People call me "old-fashioned" for my belief in an ancient and timeless teaching and for my faith in G_d. In truth, it is they who are old-fashioned, for they cling to an idea that failed decades ago.

> The Age of Reason, of Enlightenment, of Humanism—when Knowledge and Intellect were worshipped as the Redeemers of Mankind—all this died and was buried when the most civilized and intellectual nation on earth committed the most unthinking atrocities.

Rebbe Scheerson was referring to Hitler and his Nazis. However, being deeply religious, the truly venerable rebbe could not understand that, somehow, "belief systems" crept into the woodwork of the "Age of

Reason, of Enlightenment, of Humanism," for, until now, no political philosophy on earth has ever sprouted from a truly scientific theory. Had Hitler and his Nazis immersed their minds in Truth, the Holocaust would never have happened. Also, no nation on earth, not even this United States of America, has yet reached the heights of civilization in which crimes against humanity can't happen. That day is still lying millenniums in the future. When the "left column" (hypotheses and beliefs) learns to keep itself entirely separated from the "right column" (theories), peace happens naturally. This is a theory—a truth—as scientific, real, and evident as the rising and setting of the sun.

Some readers may think that I am a closet atheist or agnostic. Far from it. My personal realities include spirits and a Mother Nature who created all things. In my heart, I always feel an unshakable conviction of an unknown reality. But I have no scientific proofs that I am correct. How can I convert anyone to my own realities if I can't prove their existence? The blind have no business leading the blind. For me, just the thought of converting someone to my own ignorance is entirely unthinkable! The person who seeks to pressure people to accept unvalidated belief systems is no better than a common criminal. Each person must be free to choose his own poison or medicine, without the aggressive intervention of proselytizers for one philosophy or the other.

I am reminded of a Mexican friend who refused to let his daughter's best friend enter his home. The daughter asked, "Dad, why won't you let her come in the house?"

My friend answered, "Daughter, no one is welcome in this house, whose ignorance matches mine!"

The religions of the world are going to have to realize that the time has come for religious thinking to enter the realm of Scientific Reasoning. And this can, must, and will eventually happen. If not, Religion may cease to exist. And then the world will really be in trouble, for beliefs, hypothesis, and theories must complement each other without merging.

Here's the main secret for keeping peace in the world: Say what you want. Think what you want. Create ideas and beliefs as if they were going out of style. But if you can't convert your ideas to workable, scientific theories, don't convert anyone to your blindness. Conversions will happen automatically and naturally if some of your ideas have even a germ of merit.

An Example of How a Scientifically Verifiable Truth Can Help Clear Up Misunderstandings About Human Behavior.

Science has proven conclusively that all humans, regardless of race, are genetically identical. Only the outer shell of each human being appears to be different.

So why is crime in the United States more rampant among Blacks and Latinos than it is among Whites and Asians?

For a long time, police officers have been using what is called "racial profiling," to determine whether certain strangers roaming around in predominantly White neighborhoods should be regarded with suspicion or arrested and searched. Naturally, those "strangers" are generally Blacks and Latinos.

Recently, the legal authorities have decided to abandon racial profiling and just note the race of any person arrested. After that, this information will be used to determine "scientifically" whether a greater percentage of minorities commit crimes than Whites and Asians.

Everybody, even the Blacks and Latinos, knows what the results of these statistics will prove. They will prove that a greater number of Blacks and Latinos commit crimes than other racial groups. The result of this "racial profiling" in another Halloween mask will just confirm what everyone has known all along, with an added kick in the teeth of the Blacks and Latinos. These statistics *(beliefs disguised as science)* may effectively convince the world, even the Blacks and Latinos, that they actually *are worse than anyone else.* Are scientists wrong in concluding that everyone is alike under the skin?

If the law-enforcing organizations wanted a truly scientific way of deciding which groups are more capable of criminality than others, they would forget all about a person's color and determine his educational and occupational level. These results will show that regardless of race, the members of each educational and occupational level demonstrate approximately the same percentage of criminal tendencies. For example, if two percent of educated and occupationally superior Whites and Asians have criminal tendencies, roughly the same percentage of criminal tendencies will exist among Blacks and Latinos at the same level. If thirty percent of Blacks and Latinos with marginal educational and occupational skills have criminal tendencies, approximately thirty percent of marginal Whites and Asians will also look bad in the eyes of the Law.

We must conclude that the sicknesses of ignorance and lack of marketable skills are the true indicators of who is more likely to commit crime and exhibit undesirable moral behavior. Under the "racial" idea of who has greater criminal tendencies, the criminal elements among Whites and Asians laugh themselves silly while benefiting from the truth that a greater number of Whites and Asians have better educations and occupational skills than do Blacks and Latinos. This advantage makes it easier for them to commit crimes and stay beyond the reach of law enforcement agencies.

Ignorance and lack of marketable skills are the hallmarks of potential criminals—not skin color! That's what science can teach us. As one of my sociology professors in Mexico once told our class, "People are different only in what they carry around in their pockets and in their heads! Color and nationality don't even enter into the picture."

Mankind now finds himself at a critical crossroad in his existence. The explosion of knowledge has jumped far beyond his capacity to understand that there is no longer any logical reason for him to accept beliefs *(unproven ideas)* as gospels. But his mind still hangs on to those ogres, unwilling to let go. His primitive Genesis Self is frightened to know that once man scorns beliefs *(mental bird droppings)* as gospels by which to live and act, he forever divorces himself from his animal ancestry and becomes the partner—perhaps even the master of Nature, and no longer her victim and slave.

My heart groans in horror when I consider the continued misunderstandings and sufferings, both great and small, lying in wait for an ignorant mankind who continues to worship ignorance and gospels as beliefs.

For instance, right now, as a lover of history I'm thinking about the ignorant "politically correct" pigs who decided that the word "squaw" was an insulting epithet of Amerindian women. The truth is that the American Indians living on the East Coast of the United States derived this name for "woman" from the old Norse sailors who called their own women *Sqwam* and their homes *wigwams.* These "true believers" in political correctness, without investigating the history of the word "squaw," decided that just because the word sounded ugly in English, it was in reality an insult to Indian women. Using their political clout, they have pressured the resort of Squaw Valley, California to change its name to Olympic Valley. As a result of their ignorance and savage reliance on beliefs *(pig manure)*, mankind may never find out that this name came to America on the longboats of the Norsemen.

Of course, the people who want to prohibit Americans from using the word "squaw" don't cause nearly as much damage as the "big guys" in the game of imposing the tragedy of ignorance and beliefs *(mentally destructive ideas)* on the world.

When I first started searching for the origins of the Jews, I found evidence that they originated in ancient India. The more evidence I found, the more proofs I had that they were from India. However, when I looked up the places on ancient maps, from which the Jews originated, and from where the Bible originated, my finger always fell down on Afghanistan. "How can this be true?" I said to myself. "How can I prove to myself that the Jews were from India when the map shows that they were from Afghanistan? I'm not the best friend that the Taliban ever had." And then I realized what had gone wrong! I was trying to place the Jews in Pre-Partition India. In ancient times, Afghanistan was a part of India. Another factor hampering my research was the fundamentalist biblical thinking that humans came into existence in 5,000 BC. My mind tended to overlook evidence that humans have been here for scores of thousands of years.

Now I'm thinking of the Nazis who killed millions of innocent victims during World War II, just because they believed themselves to be "The Master Race." I'm thinking about the preacher Jim Jones who forced 900 of his followers to commit suicide at Jonestown, Guyana in 1978. I'm thinking of the Heaven's Gate sect near San Diego, California, who in 1997 thought that by committing suicide, they would board the Hale-Bopp comet for parts unknown. I'm thinking of the mass killer Timothy McVeigh who also in 1997 blew 167 innocent victims to smithereens in Oklahoma City, just because he hated the government. You may want to point out that these are extreme examples of the potential destructiveness of ignorance and beliefs *(mind crime)*. But that's because most of us are accustomed to living in ignorance and accepting beliefs *(mental poverty)* as gospel truths. How can a savage living in the heart of the jungles of Brazil know that there are better ways to think and live if he has never been exposed to them?

What you may not know is that *RIGHT NOW* you are doing a combination *Nazi Hitlerian holocaust, mafia, and Jim Jones job* on yourself— every day of your life! In many cases, you have bought the "believe in yourself" myth, convincing yourself that you can do such and such—or be such and such—without the knowledge you need to be successful in areas that interest you. Perhaps you have used "negative belief" to convince yourself that you don't have what it takes to accomplish great things in life.

Don't you think it's time to wake up?

How many more injustices will be perpetrated upon the earth and all the beings in it, as long as even a few diehards keep hanging on to ignorance and gospel-like beliefs *(devil worship)* as lifelines?

I know of no other word than "belief," that carries so much potential to destroy individuals and nations. As the knowledge explosion continues to grow, that word will no longer be able to hide the one hundred percent proven truth that it a monster.

Author Jon Baron, in his book *Rationality and Intelligence,* defines the essence of intelligence as the art of rational thinking—a talent anyone can learn:

> Most people...rely on some 'authority' to tell them what's right...they should be more critical of the first ideas that pop into their heads...Teaching people to think rationally will make them more intelligent.

Mr. Baron probably didn't know, when he wrote his famous book, that "thinking rationally" is basically no more difficult than realizing that "belief" is mankind's most elemental and primitive way of thinking. Once people stop booting it over to the knowledge side of the modern *homo sapiens sapiens* thinking spectrum, the problem of getting people to think rationally will be largely solved!

Mankind's intelligence and moral life will continue to be found wanting as long as the frankenstinian monster called *Belief* remains enthroned in the human soul. Had human demons like Adolph Hitler looked up the meaning of *Belief* in their dictionaries, the holocaust might never have happened. We must deal with that monster now, before it is too late. I pray that my readers have learned enough in this book to understand fully that once *Belief* gets straitjacketed—*intelligence happens!*

Are you satisfied with what you are carrying around in your head and in your pocket? If not, start, right now, to triple your efforts in all areas—especially those required to keep *Belief* chained forever in Hell.

Practice ridding yourself of the tyranny of beliefs.

Unlike many bad habits plaguing the lives of human beings, almost anyone can free himself from slavery to his beliefs. The reason for this is that nearly all of us can agree one hundred percent on the dictionary definition. Besides, Man has never been more ready than he is now to make this gigantic leap away from his primitive jungle self! Through a little practice, anyone can weaken the hold of beliefs *(Neanderthal thinking)* on his soul.

Ideally, the schoolroom is the ideal place to educate people to keep beliefs and hypotheses on the left side of the column. But such a luxury may never happen in the immediate future. Selfish interests and the ruling powers are probably still reluctant to lose their slaves. Therefore, you may have to practice on your own.

If you have any family members, friends, or acquaintances interested in becoming citizens of the future, you can practice together: purposely debating, arguing, etc., until you get to the point where you understand that beliefs *(chicken clucks)* are certainly nothing to get excited about.

Better still, keep company with people who are in love with their ideas and want to push them off on you. Look for opportunities to engage them in debate and conversation. When you both get to the point where things are getting hot and heavy, *concede*. Tell your opponent that your arguments can in no way match his. Say things like, "I have absolutely no scientific authority to prove that my ideas are superior to yours. By your own passionate devotion to your ideas, I can do no more than infer that you have access to valid authoritative sources. I don't have that luxury. Therefore, you win the day."

When you concede, a person wanting to cram his religious or political ideas down your throat may demand that you prove your sincerity by converting. In this case, you can say, "I'm sorry, but I still like being a lost soul. However, I'll certainly keep you in mind whenever I start feeling spiritually empty. You certainly have presented some convincing arguments to me."

Keep in mind the importance of *always conceding; always conceding; always conceding.* Always give in to your antagonist in debates and arguments brought about by *Belief.* Always claim to be the "loser." And why not? By winning a debate based on belief, you are actually saying, "You're correct. I want to be the same kind of fool you are." Who wants to live his life as if it were a lie? The truth is that there are never any winners of debates, discussions, arguments, political negotiations, religious arguments, and other similar traps that have been set by the savage, primitive hunter named *Belief.* Both sides lose! Don't forget: each time you are tempted to defend your beliefs *(insane screams)* or challenge those of someone else, the Neanderthal caveman in every human heart is fighting to reincarnate itself.

Just as you would be careful wherever you step in rattlesnake country, always be wary, but not fearful, of that rattlesnake called "belief." Whenever you meet someone for the first time, say to yourself: *"Behind those eyes there's a force deciding what I am and what to do about me."* When you look into the eyes of someone you know well, say to yourself: *"Behind those eyes there's a force that has already decided."* The fearful thing is that it may not let you know *what it will decide or has decided.*

I'll never forget when I was living in San Jose, Costa Rica during the late 1950s. The Costa Rican government permitted a famous Marxist political activist and exile to return home. At that time in history, Costa Rica had only a million inhabitants. The man was allowed to give a speech in San Jose's *Plaza Central* on May 1, a major holiday of the international Marxist movement. Two hundred fifty thousand people, twenty-five percent of the country's population, gathered in that plaza. He spent part of the afternoon preaching fiery hate for Americans. While I was standing amidst that throng, many people would gaze at me, unable to hide the hostility behind those eyes. Don't forget: they were being indoctrinated to believe; not to know! I was lucky to leave that plaza alive.

If you ever find yourself in an extreme situation, such as the one I had to contend with on that first day of May, use every known strategy to encourage the force behind those eyes—if it exercises some degree of power over you—not to reinforce attitudes and make decisions detrimental to your happiness, progress and well-being. In most cases it's just a bully—if the person looking at you is all by himself. Make it fearful of what you may or may not decide about it! You can—and should—do it. But if you find yourself in the middle of a hostile group, such I was that day, I hope you are a good runner. I present this story from the pages of my own past life as an illustration of the potential evils lurking beyond many human beliefs.

You must also decide whether or not it really matters what that force behind people's eyes believes and decides where you're concerned. If keeping it at bay means that you should be a coward and deny yourself whatever honorable and harmless behaviors make you happy, thumb your nose at it. When a principal of the high school where I once taught told me that many of my *gringo* colleagues hated me for going to Mexican dances, speaking Spanish all the time, and spending more time with Mexicans than with them, I answered, "Now, ask my if I care. Those bible-belt teachers are all assholes anyway!"

Perhaps you are thinking about now: "If I went around wondering what lies behind all those eyes looking at me in private and public gatherings, I might become paranoid." This is my comment: "My friend, forget about that word 'might.' If you could really hear the thoughts milling around behind all those eyes, you *WOULD* become paranoid!" This is one of the major reasons why I wrote this book. We *MUST* learn how to think rationally.

As I have implied throughout this book, mankind has outgrown the need to even use the "B" word any more. *Belief* has become obsolete—an anachronism—a dinosaur. Its companion words, such as *think, suspect, am convinced, opine, guess, etc.,* often, but not always, fail to inspire strong positive or negative emotions. By trashing this word *belief*, we may also trash problems and misunderstandings that no longer have any place in modern living. As a life-long training exercise, why not try using this word as little as possible the rest of your life? I also *opine* that the demise of *skepticism* would benefit mankind immeasurably.

Here are a few more examples among those already given of how to defang the poison of beliefs *(mental putrefaction)*:

Instead of saying, "I believe that the rich should give all of their money to the poor," say what's really on your mind: *I wish that rich people would share their fortunes with me.*

"I believe you are a criminal." Change this to, *My guess is that your honesty is not up to par.*

Instead of looking a person in the face and saying, "You are the Devil incarnate," say, *You are Devil-may-care in your interrelationships.*

Do you get the hint? Don't be emphatic about events and things you can't prove.

You have everything to gain and nothing to lose by refusing to *believe* any more! For example, after finishing this book, a reader may say, "I've read Mr. Matlock's book and determined that *I don't believe a word he said.*" If a person says that upon finishing this book, I've failed with him miserably, for *I don't believe* is the same as *I believe not.* Yes, you guessed it. *He's still a believer! He believes—not.* Wherever yes-beliefs and not-beliefs are concerned, neutrality is always a safe mindset. However, you'll often encounter arguments about ideas and things that may attract you. As long as you keep in mind that if they are not proven truths like electricity and the world we live in, you're still on safe ground. Just make sure that you don't get excited and apprehensive if others don't share your enthusiasm. You should not even care what a person thinks about an event or thing if what you are doing or recommending has no universally accepted validity. Why? It is scientifically true and valid that *belief* does not suggest *truth.*

Let's suppose that another reader closes this book upon finishing it, exclaiming, "I've read this book with an open mind and determined that *I can't accept what Mr. Matlock has taught.*" In this case, I have still failed miserably in getting my message across, *for I have turned the reader into a bare-faced liar.* He has said, "I don't accept the dictionary definition of belief." The total agenda of this book is to teach readers the difference between belief and truth. Surely, in a 40,000 words plus document, such as this one, I have convinced someone to learn the definitions of these two words—once and for all time!

Here's an exercise that you must practice for the weeks, months, or years to keep the boxers *Belief* and *Truth* in their respective corners. Read what comes next, thinking about it deeply, until it becomes welded in your soul.

Truth does not generally generate negative, potentially destructive emotions and situations. It is self-evident. When Belief begins to merge with the Truth side, the individual unconsciously realizes that he can't maintain it where it doesn't belong. Therefore, when his beliefs or self-imposed delusions are challenged, or don't meet his expectations, he consciously and unconsciously struggles to keep them there by any means possible—even if that means he must delude himself. Each time you notice the least bit of resentment or frustration welling up in your being when your beliefs fail to perform as truths, train yourself to calm down and not to force the unreal on your consciousness and those around you. When a person tries to force his beliefs to appear as truths, the damage to his psyche is so great that even his physical health suffers as well. Nature doesn't want people to take their beliefs too seriously!

Read what I have said in the preceding paragraph over and over again, meditating deeply about the necessity of keeping Belief separate from Truth, until you achieve success.

TRIPLING YOUR EFFORTS = TRIPLING YOUR INTELLIGENCE!
BECOME BETTER THAN EVERYBODY ELSE!
ABANDON BELIEFS. SEARCH FOR TRUTH.

IF YOU HAVE KNOWLEDGE OF SOMETHING, AND CAN'T PROVE ITS REALITY TO OTHERS WITH DEMONSTRABLE PROOFS AND SIGNS, YOUR SO-CALLED "TRUTH" IS NO BETTER THAN A BELIEF. DON'T CONVERT ANYONE TO SOMETHING ONLY YOU AND A FEW OTHERS KNOW UNTIL YOU CAN PROVE ITS VALIDITY TO EVERYBODY. DON'T CONVERT. SHOW DEMONSTRABLE PROOF.

Compared to what I have taught about *Belief* in this book, all the other teachings and advice are just "fill-in" in order to make a document called "book." Once a person has been trained to separate beliefs from valid truths, his mental ability rockets skyward! At the same time, he will become much more receptive to knowledge because the mind no longer welds itself to non-realities. If anyone has been looking for a "magical formula for intelligence enhancement" all his life, he need look no further. This is it.

The End

About the Author

Since he could barely crawl, Gene D. Matlock had been battered on all sides that some big changes would come about in this world immediately after everyone started shouting "Happy New Year," just after midnight, on January 1, 2001. Even as a young man, he understood that if beneficial changes were to come about, mankind would have to start working on that mess he calls "Belief" and start becoming more preoccupied with "Truth." This preoccupation led to the writing of the following books:

Jesus and Moses Are Buried in India, Birthplace of Abraham and the Hebrews!

Yishvara 2000—The Hindu Ancestor of Judaism Speaks to This Millennium.

India Once Ruled the Americas.

The Last Atlantis Book You'll Ever Have to Read!

From Khyber (Kheeber) Pass to Gran Quivira (Kheevira), NM and Baboquivari, AZ—When India Ruled the World!

And, of course, the book you've just finished.

9 780595 199754

47574415R00088

Made in the USA
San Bernardino, CA
03 April 2017